Daniel P. Johnson

Sustaining Change in Schools

HOW TO OVERCOME DIFFERENCES AND FOCUS ON QUALITY

Association for Supervision
and Curriculum Development
Alexandria, Virginia USA

Association for Supervision and Curriculum Development
1703 N. Beauregard St. • Alexandria, VA 22311-1714 USA
Phone: 800-933-2723 or 703-578-9600 • Fax: 703-575-5400
Web site: www.ascd.org • E-mail: member@ascd.org
Author guidelines: www.ascd.org/write

Gene R. Carter, *Executive Director;* Nancy Modrak, *Director of Publishing;* Julie Houtz, *Director of Book Editing & Production;* Ernesto Yermoli, *Project Manager;* Georgia Park, *Senior Graphic Designer;* Cynthia Stock, *Typesetter;* Vivian Coss, *Production Specialist*

Printed in the United States of America. Cover art copyright © 2005 by ASCD. ASCD publications present a variety of viewpoints. The views expressed or implied in this book should not be interpreted as official positions of the Association.

ASCD Member Book, No. FY05-7 (May 2005, P). ASCD Member Books mail to Premium (P), Comprehensive (C), and Regular (R) members on this schedule: Jan., PC; Feb., P; Apr., PCR; May, P; July, PC; Aug., P; Sept., PCR; Nov., PC; Dec., P.

Paperback ISBN: 1-4166-0147-3 • ASCD product #105006 • List Price: $25.95
 ($19.95 ASCD member price, direct from ASCD only)

e-books ($25.95): retail PDF ISBN: 1-4166-0256-9 • netLibrary ISBN: 1-4166-0254-2 •
 ebrary ISBN: 1-4166-0255-0

Quantity discounts for the paperback book: 10–49 copies, 10%; 50+ copies, 15%; for 500 or more copies, call 800-933-2723, ext. 5634, or 703-575-5634.

Library of Congress Cataloging-in-Publication Data

Johnson, Daniel P.
    Sustaining change in schools : how to overcome differences and focus on quality / Daniel P. Johnson.
        p.   cm.
    Includes bibliographical references.
    ISBN 1-4166-0147-3 (alk. paper)
    1. School management and organization—United States. 2. Educational leadership—United States. 3. Typology (Psychology) I. Title.

    LB2806.J584 2005
    371.2'00973—dc22

                                                                2005002845

12 11 10 09 08 07 06 05   12 11 10 9 8 7 6 5 4 3 2 1

Sustaining Change in Schools

Foreword

The spring of 2000 marked a turning point for the Thompson School District. It was then that we began to understand the power of the opening words of our mission statement: "In partnership with the community." We did more than ask our stakeholders what they believed students needed to know and be able to do; we asked them how they would know when we had reached those goals. What would students be doing? What would staff be doing? What would parents be doing? Then we asked them what they were willing to commit to make that happen. Finally, we asked the four main questions outlined in this book:

- Why is this important for a student to know or be able to do?
- What do we have in place to make that happen?
- How will we adjust what is in place so that it works for all students?
- To what extent are we supporting programs and services that work?

Each of us asks these questions in our own words. Perhaps that's what makes them so powerful. They have given us a practical process to focus on what works for kids.

We all have our own special beliefs and philosophies, but now we spend less time arguing about them. Instead, we ask to see data on student progress. And we don't want to see only one data source—our staff and parent advisory committees recognize that the school board will not make major budget decisions without first examining data on what is working for students and how it contributes to success for all of them.

We don't expect our questions to uncover a silver bullet that will fix every problem in our school district. But we have reached a point where we can recognize what is working and what is not. Building staffs and advisory committees throughout the community are setting goals and painting clear targets for multiple groups of students. Our biggest struggle now is getting good information into as many hands as possible.

We still have plenty of disagreements. But we are developing a new sense of trust. Posturing until you get what you want is being replaced by a sense of community and a sense of questioning. We are asking questions together and sharing our answers publicly, becoming true partners with our community. This partnership gives me hope that my years on the school board have made a difference and that we are on the right track.

It is truly amazing what you can learn when you ask the right questions. You may ask them differently than we ask them in our school district. But once you understand the power of asking the right questions, you'll spend far less time arguing about procedures and far more time thinking about what students are learning and what you can do to help them all succeed.

Becky Jay, Board President
Thompson School District
Loveland, Colorado

Introduction

The superintendent sits quietly as seven school board members decide the future of the Thompson School District. Jay, the president, is an impatient neurologist who makes life-or-death decisions on a daily basis. Clark is a quality control engineer who makes most of his decisions based on a closed-loop analysis of data. Donna and Maria are former teachers who want people to be excited about working in the Thompson Schools. Judy, who teaches preschool, expresses her passion for developmentally appropriate teaching practices in a competent, unassuming manner. Bonnie and Trisha's continued involvement with school accountability committees has made them strong advocates for parent and community involvement in all major school district decisions.

Tonight is the final meeting before the school board adopts the district's annual budget—approximately $100 million. It has been a difficult spring. School funding has followed the economy into a spiraling decline, teacher negotiations have been acrimonious, and the pace of change over the past three years has overwhelmed almost everyone. Nevertheless, these seven lay citizens are about to decide which of the $1.4 million worth of program and service priorities will be funded from only $400,000 in available new revenues.

In the audience are a number of anxious middle school teachers and parents who have been attending school board meetings for several months

1

during a rigorous middle school program review. Scattered throughout this group are lead principals from the elementary, middle, and high school levels, along with the superintendent's executive team and several district office program directors. They listen intently as the board members shape their budget rationale from seven individual opinions into a board decision.

After 30 minutes of discussion, the school board members give the superintendent direction regarding how they want to allocate resources for the coming year. Board members listen to a few audience comments and adjourn the meeting. A few parents and staff members stop to thank the board members for being conscientious in their deliberations, open to input from all stakeholder groups, and courageous in making the tough decisions.

In the midst of these problems, how did these seven lay citizens from various backgrounds agree on a plan for funding their schools? How did they find a way to close the gap between purpose and practice in their school district? And how will the school board's decisions affect the quality of the district's schools?

This book outlines a change process that was used by the Thompson School District in Loveland, Colorado. The process has evolved over a 25-year period across four school districts and three states, and it can be used by school leaders everywhere to move their community five steps closer to quality schools.

The five steps are as follows:

Step 1: Understanding the quality profile
Step 2: Asking quality questions
Step 3: Making quality a habit
Step 4: Focusing on success
Step 5: Managing tasks and leading people

The first five chapters of this guide explain each of these five steps, using practical examples and presenting practical tools for promoting and sustaining quality schools over time and across groups and communities. The final chapter describes how you can nurture quality leadership in your own school district.

Chapter 1 identifies the Four *P*s of leadership and management: purpose, parameters, principles, and priorities. The Four *P*s provide a link between individual personality traits and those of a school district; by linking the two, you can learn to manage ongoing organizational tasks so that your school community begins to see differences as assets rather than roadblocks.

Chapter 2 explores four critical attributes of a connected learning community that shift decision making from a political exercise to a data-driven one—an inquiry based on four critical questions related to each of the Four *P*s. You will learn how to adapt these questions to create a connected learning community.

Chapter 3 considers four management protocols—strategic planning, shared decision making, accountability, and funding priorities—and how you can use them to link day-to-day tasks to the school district's strategic goals.

Chapter 4 describes various stakeholders' responsibilities for sustaining quality at all levels. In this chapter, we'll explore how stakeholders can learn to focus on success. You will also learn how to evaluate existing practices to align them with changing expectations for student achievement and well-being.

Chapter 5 presents ways to analyze and align tasks so that they become a means to an end rather than taking on a life of their own. You will learn to use a task analysis checklist to manage daily tasks toward success for *all* students.

Finally, Chapter 6 explores leadership as a partnership. In this chapter, you will consider the challenges of changing the way you think about leaders and leadership so that communities can sustain quality public schools over time and across groups and communities.

Leaders—whether teachers, principals, central office staff, or school board members—will find these practical processes and organizational structures useful in moving school districts five steps closer to quality. Our democracy depends on strong public schools, and strong public schools depend on strong partnerships among school district stakeholders. This guide describes how these partnerships can be created and sustained.

1

Understanding the
Quality Profile

Quality is a shifting target defined by people's perceptions.

No matter what standards the public schools achieve, their quality depends on how much the community values their product. To sustain quality over time and across groups and communities, school leaders need to understand what people value. We need to be aware of how parents, staff, and other community stakeholders define quality at any point in time.

I became interested in people's perceptions of public institutions in the 1970s. President Nixon's resignation in August of 1974 seemed to symbolize the inability of public institutions to respond effectively to a changing world. Toffler's (1970) prediction of a "future shock" of rapid technological change was upon us. In the midst of this tumult stood a public school system that had been designed for the industrial needs of the early 20th century—oh, that shifting target.

My dissertation committee at the time showed little interest in what I then referred to as the "emotional" side of change. The committee recognized, as I did, that people embrace progress but loathe change. I was eventually permitted to conduct a descriptive study of the "gaps between what schools [were] actually accomplishing and what [students, educators, and society thought] schools ought to be accomplishing" (Johnson, 1980). I used this needs assessment and strategic planning theory throughout my early administrative career, but I remained convinced that somewhere within what Galpin (1996) later called "the human side of change" lay a missing link—a link necessary to define and accomplish quality in the public schools.

As an administrator, I implemented effective change processes at the building level into the mid-1980s. Then, in the 1990s, I discovered that implementation was the easy part—sustaining meaningful change across groups and communities was the difficulty. This epiphany came during my involvement with the Third International Mathematics and Science Study (TIMSS) (Kroeze & Johnson, 1997), during which I noticed two key findings: (1) the significant correlation between adult expectations and student performance, and (2) the mismatch between purpose and practice in U.S. classrooms.

Figure 1.1 summarizes a key finding from the TIMSS results. These results indicated that throughout the world, adult expectations, particularly those of parents, were the single most significant factor related to students' academic performance. But of equal interest to me was the gap between how U.S. mathematics teachers had intended to teach their content and what TIMSS researchers actually observed in their classroom practices. In interviews prior to the study, U.S. mathematics teachers told TIMSS researchers that they were implementing the National Council of Teachers of Mathematics (NCTM) standards. But when trained researchers later observed mathematics classrooms throughout the United States, they saw very few signs of the standards in daily practice.

Were U.S. teachers lying to observers? Were they consciously or subconsciously avoiding the NCTM standards? Were they lazy or unmotivated? Were they incompetent?

I had known too many teachers during my 25 years in education to attribute these negative motives to members of our profession. Of course, U.S. mathematics and science standards needed to be more clearly articulated. But how could TIMSS researchers explain the fact that articulated standards were common in both high- and low-performing schools throughout the world?

FIGURE 1.1 Purpose vs. Practice in Math Classrooms	
Purpose	Practice
Teaching all students to think mathematically	Teaching some students to remember math facts and procedures

Of course, teachers and administrators needed training. But the TIMSS results indicated a need for something more than training in mathematics and science content. Of course, expectations for student performance needed to be raised. But how could we raise standards for student performance if teachers were not able to match intent with practice?

Following several more years of painstaking analyses, I returned to personality and group dynamics as the missing link to sustaining quality public schools. I found a bridge across the chasm between purpose and practice as I considered similarities between Bolman and Deal's (1984, 1997) research and Keirsey and Bates's (1978, 1998) research into personality. Bolman and Deal's research indicates that organizational cultures function both for and because of people. Keirsey and Bates's research indicates that numerous cultural factors inhibit individuals from fully developing their skills and talents. Bolman and Deal identify four aspects of school culture: human resource, symbolic, strategic, and political. Keirsey and Bates identify four personality types: Idealist, Guardian, Rational, and Artisan.

The link between these two bodies of research lies in what I have come to call the Four Ps: **purpose, parameters, principles,** and **priorities.** All individuals and organizations have the ability to deal with the world through the Four Ps, but they typically emphasize one or two of these personality characteristics over the others. When this happens, the quality of their work and the quality of their lives suffer. The irony in this situation is that balancing the Four Ps has as much to do with letting go of what we do well as it does with overcoming our liabilities. For example, people or organizations that become fixed on standards and rules (*parameters*) may lose sight of their intended goals (*purpose*); conversely, people or organizations that become fixed on human relations (*purpose*) may initially make everyone happy but ultimately fail to produce anything that people value at that moment (*priorities*). Whether individually or within an organizational culture, quality depends on a dynamic balance among the Four *P*s, as shown in Figure 1.2.

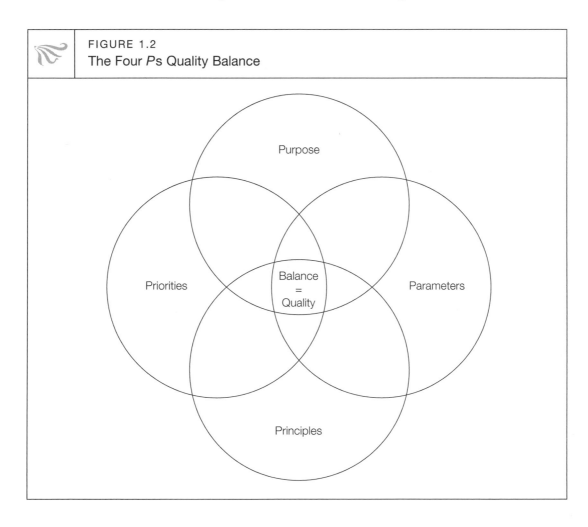

FIGURE 1.2
The Four *P*s Quality Balance

Purpose

Priorities

Balance
=
Quality

Parameters

Principles

School leaders must engage in a complicated juggling act to provide this dynamic balance. Effective leaders help stakeholders build a common purpose for learning. They manage organizational structures so that stakeholders can focus on short-term needs without losing sight of long-term goals. They support decision-making parameters that articulate change efforts from the classroom to the boardroom. They help stakeholders align daily practice with a deep and abiding set of principles based on success for all students. Finally, they help stakeholders leverage available resources to achieve specific organizational priorities.

This guide is the result of 25 years of research and practice into what leaders can do to create and sustain quality schools. Although I cite examples of the Four *P*s from across the country, most of my examples are drawn from the Thompson School District in Loveland, Colorado. The Thompson community has implemented and supported the Four *P*s systemically over the past four years. As you read about the Four *P*s in action and think about your own school or school district, ask yourself the following questions:

- Do my stakeholders know and trust one another enough to discuss their expectations for quality schools openly and honestly?
- Have we created mechanisms for individuals and groups to discuss their expectations and to make effective decisions about how to pursue quality schools?
- Do we align our daily practices with the principles underlying our stated purpose for schools and learning?
- Do we act on our priorities or simply talk about them?

You can use these questions as a school leader to develop a clear picture of quality in your own setting. They are questions that every teacher, administrator, parent, and school board member should ask on a regular basis. Use them to clarify your target for quality schools, first as individuals, and then as a community. Use them to decide when to move the quality target rather than simply allowing it to be moved for you. Use them to monitor programs and services to determine how closely your daily practices align with your stated principles. Use them to set priorities that can make your expectations more attainable. Use them to change the way you and your community think about quality schools.

Changing the Way We Think About Change

The public schools work for many students; in fact, they work for most students at various points in time. But school leaders are responsible for making schools work effectively for *all* students most of the time.

Figure 1.3 illustrates that school leaders should use the Four *Ps* to focus attention on learning, rather than teaching, to achieve quality. By reflecting on learning across all organizational structures, adults can model the behaviors they want students to develop.

Learning experiences can be divided into two groups: those that achieve expected results (if I do X, I will probably get Y), and those that enhance the possibility of different results (I wonder what might happen if I do X). The bottom half of Figure 1.3 illustrates what happens when individuals or groups engage with their world through multiple learning experiences, and the top half illustrates how individuals and groups connect these experiences to make sense of their world.

Let's use the example of infants to illustrate the points of Figure 1.3. Babies learn that if they cry long enough and loud enough, adults will respond in some way. Based on these experiences, babies quickly develop parameters for managing their environment to enhance the probability that their actions will achieve expected results (lower left bubble). However, as babies have more and more experiences within their environment, they begin to notice slightly different results from one experience to another, and to consider multiple possibilities for gaining control over their environment (bottom right bubble). For example, babies learn quickly that they can cry to express their choices among various foods (fruits versus vegetables) as a means of increasing the possibilities (choices) within their environment.

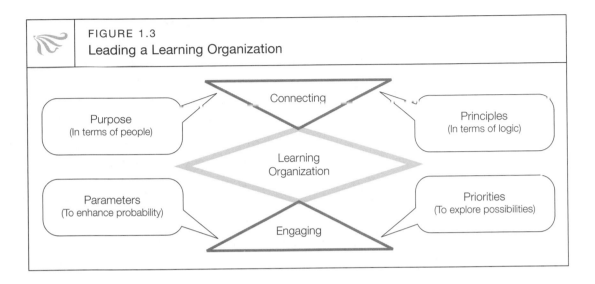

FIGURE 1.3
Leading a Learning Organization

Connecting

Purpose
(In terms of people)

Principles
(In terms of logic)

Learning
Organization

Parameters
(To enhance probability)

Priorities
(To explore possibilities)

Engaging

Babies watch the people around them for clues about how the world works (top left bubble) and connect those clues into patterns or principles of human interaction (top right bubble). When babies cry long enough and loud enough, Mom and Dad are likely to give them what they want, but strangers may walk away. Within a very short time, babies develop principles to regulate their tantrums according to their needs and their audience. They learn to analyze their actions and their results to determine how they want to allocate their efforts to meet future needs.

These are the same factors that drive learning in groups and organizations. Quality classroom learning experiences require a certain amount of collaboration among students, parents, and teachers. As the learning environment grows larger to include departments, grade levels, school sites, and the district, possibilities—both for success and for failure—grow exponentially. Departments and grade levels require teamwork; school sites require students, parents, and staff to function as a community of learners; and schools need to network with one another within their levels (elementary, middle, and high schools) in order to ensure that the district can function as a focused learning community.

The diamond in the center of Figure 1.3 illustrates what Senge (1990) calls a learning organization—an alignment between a community's expectations for student learning and the behaviors of the adults who plan for and implement learning experiences within the school. School leaders can use the Four *P*s to align the ways in which district stakeholders plan for, manage, analyze, and allocate resources for learning with the ways in which individual students learn. Leaders can create a learning organization that models effective learning to meet students' individual needs. As stakeholder groups come to understand their responsibilities within this process, they can make their voices heard and influence the purpose and direction of various tasks.

The quality of a school district depends on the stakeholders' ability to use and expand their existing talents in order to meet students' needs—hitting the target more consistently over time. It also depends on their ability to reflect on learning. Unfortunately, educators often become fixed on standards (parameters) to the detriment of the remaining *P*s: purpose, principles, and priorities. They do what they do effectively, but stakeholders may not value their efforts. Quality emerges logically from the school district's purpose, is guided by accepted decision-making parameters, adheres to principles of learning and teaching that meet students' needs, and points the way to future actions that can sustain that quality over time and across groups and communities.

Change is not simply about doing what we do better, changing everything we do, switching those involved in implementing the change, or modifying how the change is implemented. It is about rethinking how goals, programs, and services fit together to keep pace with a changing world. Changing our public schools is a qualitative issue rather than a compliance issue. Figure 1.4 illustrates that change involves both products and processes.

The TIMSS findings suggest that school leaders cannot simply declare a change in attitudes or behaviors across a school community. To change teaching, leaders must first change people's understanding of learning. We talk about learning differences, but do we really understand them? Do school district stakeholders understand that while people use all the Four *P*s to learn,

FIGURE 1.4 Connecting the Four Faces of Change	
Product	**Process**
More knowledge and skills	Interactions with *people*
New knowledge and skills	Interactions with *ideas*

they don't necessarily use them in the same order? Do they understand that differences in this order can create significant disparities in how people define quality in schools or in any other setting? And do they have the ability to recognize and respond effectively to these differences in order to paint a clear target for the change process—a learning target?

Joe is a middle school principal whose parent advisory group actively supports a goal to improve the quality of the math program over the next three years. What Joe does not understand, however, is what that quality looks like to four different members of the group. To Raul, the father of a gifted 7th grade student, it means creating a higher track of math so that his daughter can take algebra this year. He sympathizes with children who might fall into lower track math classes, but he wants his daughter to be challenged academically. Tammy, however, is an engineer who judges quality by whether students love math and show interest in math-related careers. Bob, who believes himself to be poor at math, would be happy if his daughter could calculate the correct change at a grocery store. And Jenny is less interested in math than in her son's social development at what she sees as this critical developmental period in his life. And the target looks like . . . ?

Piaget (1977) suggests that humans learn by dealing with some degree of dissonance between what they already believe and what they confront in new situations. However, according to Hart (1983), when individuals are placed in a situation that becomes too threatening, they experience "downshifting," an actual physiological state that Caine and Caine (1991) suggest is "accompanied by a sense of helplessness and lack of self-efficacy." Consequently, school leaders need to manage tasks in a way that lets stakeholders engage with change rather than feel threatened by it. This balance provides a frame of reference for continuous quality schools.

Quality schools grow and thrive when people have opportunities for ongoing discussions within an environment that values and respects differences; they promote and respect differences at every level, so that staff and parents model the types of learning they want students to achieve in their classrooms; and they require an understanding of people's attitudes and beliefs about learning. Armed with this insight, school leaders can manage organizational structures to address various perceptions of quality.

Leading People

Experts differ on the precise definition of learning and the processes through which it occurs. Piaget (1952) describes learning in terms of a reasonably consistent set of developmental stages through which all individuals progress; Skinner (1948, 1968) describes it as a matter of shaping behavior through controlled consequences. Gardner (1993) focuses on both the purpose and the nature of learning, suggesting that educators need to be aware of and intent on developing learners through multiple intelligences. Through recent advancements in brain imaging technology, many experts have switched their emphasis from describing what intelligence is to describing how thinking occurs.

The common thread among these different learning theories is that individuals learn by engaging with their world and drawing connections among their experiences. Learning is about making connections with people and ideas—connections that function as both the means and the ends of learning. The more we practice our beliefs and compare the results of our experiences with others, the more effective we become as learners. We learn to connect with other people (especially those who think differently than we do) in order to gain the most from and contribute the most to our world.

Let's take a closer look at the Four *P*s as they emerge through individual personalities. By understanding these personality differences, we can learn to form partnerships that thrive on differences rather than avoid them.

The Four *P*s and Individuals

Although numerous models have been devised to clarify and simplify personality concepts, these models tend to have more similarities than differences. My concept of the Four *P*s is based on research as ancient as Plato's (340 B.C.) and as recent as Myers and McCaulley's (1985) and Keirsey and Bates's (1998). The Four *P*s provide a practical lens through which ordinary people can examine how they process information and interact with one another.

Human beings cannot simply be categorized into personality types. Life is too complicated for that. But we have learned from years of research that people tend to lead with one of the Four *P*s prior to considering the other three. As Frankl (1959) indicates, all individuals search for meaning or a purpose in their lives. They function within some sense of reasonable parameters according to general principles (either moral or logical) of right and wrong. They set certain priorities in their lives to balance what they want with what is available to them within their existing environment.

Let's look first at how the Four *P*s—purpose, parameters, principles, and priorities—apply to individuals, and then examine how they apply to school districts as a whole.

Purpose

The purpose question asks, "Why is this important?" It focuses on people. From our earliest childhood years, we recognize and seek connections with the people around us. Eventually, this need to belong leads us to accept or believe in some higher purpose. To some, this is a collective physical purpose; to others, it may be a mysterious metaphysical purpose. But while all human beings ask the purpose question, each of us attaches different degrees of significance to the effect of the question on our daily lives. According to

Keirsey and Bates (1998), the purpose question guides some people's thinking more than others. Keirsey and Bates's research indicates that approximately 10 percent of human beings approach most learning experiences from this perspective—how their actions and experiences affect or are affected by their relationships with other people.

Cynthia is a mother who sees life as fundamentally a matter of human relationships. The question of purpose—"Why is this important?"—drives her thoughts and actions. As a learner, she is what Keirsey and Bates refer to as an **Idealist**, an abstract cooperator, or an intuitive-feeling learner. Cynthia can make small talk as easily with my school board president, who is a neurologist, as she can with my brother, who has spent his career as a trucker. She loathes descriptions of people that depend on their occupation. She approaches every person in the same way, sensing what is important to them and immediately creating and sustaining connections. She ignores protocol in favor of *purpose*. She has an uncanny ability to connect with the people around her, to see the world through their eyes. She is both incredulous and exasperated with people who cannot establish such connections.

Parameters

The parameters question asks, "What are the rules of engagement?" Again, even the youngest of children look for clues that define what is or is not acceptable to family, friends, and significant others. They focus on experiences as opportunities to draw them closer to the group. We all want to know what people expect of us, how accountable we are to those expectations, and how our responsibilities compare to those of the people around us. But while all individuals ask parameter questions, Keirsey and Bates's research indicates that approximately 45 to 50 percent of us see parameters as the most important of the Four *P*s. In general, these individuals believe that people could exist more harmoniously with one another if they understood and lived by the rules of the game.

Keiko, a central office administrator, is what Keirsey and Bates refer to as a **Guardian.** She is concrete in her view of the world—a concrete cooperator, or sensing-judging learner. There is no one better than Keiko at analyzing a task. If I go to Keiko for advice, she will ask, "What three things do you want people to know or be able to do as a result of what you are doing?" Then she will walk me through a series of questions until I can list my three points clearly and succinctly. Keiko is a logistics expert who can analyze a task, limit the information in appropriate ways for her audience, and organize learning activities in a way that is both informative and practical. As a leader and a learner, Keiko is an effective manager who gets results.

Principles

The principles question asks, "How do I make this work?" The principle-oriented individual recognizes that each person and each situation differs from those that have come before and those that might follow. While we all ask the principles question at various points in our lives, Keirsey and Bates (1998) indicate that only 5 to 10 percent of us consistently make connections among experiences on the basis of their fit with logical principles; many individuals and groups simply accept the rules of the game or see them as too overwhelming or too entrenched to be altered.

Jason is what Keirsey and Bates refer to as a **Rational.** He is an intuitive-thinking learner, as opposed to an intuitive-feeling one. He finds working with people to be a challenge. He has the ability to remove himself from personal connections, attending more to ideas and principles that can improve the human condition. Jason's goals are no less noble than Cynthia's; he simply approaches the world with a different question. This motivation drove him to become a physician.

People who know Jason on a personal level see him as a caring person. But those who work with him professionally don't always get beyond the very direct, sometimes abrupt manner in which he solves problems. Jason, who serves on a school board, can at times be a bit of a rebel. He often asks tough questions of the superintendent or other board members. When others tell him in private that they are surprised or offended by his dogged interrogations, he is most often genuinely surprised. He views his questions as simply a way of getting at the facts. He would say that people are just too thin-skinned, and that he has an obligation to his constituents to make certain he has all the information before making a decision.

Priorities

The priorities question asks, "Will this make a difference?" This is the question that approximately 35 to 40 percent of the world's population sees as the most important of the Four *P*s (Keirsey & Bates, 1998). Priorities people act according to what they know (or sometimes in spite of what they don't know).

Maria is what Keirsey and Bates refer to as an **Artisan.** She is a concrete utilitarian, or sensing-perceiving learner. Like Keiko, she approaches problems from a very concrete perspective. She values facts and events as opportunities to discover and meet immediate needs. Maria is a school district finance officer, and her financial reports are generally outlined in a manner that is much more accessible to nonfinancial minds than those many finance officers produce. At the same time, she occasionally gives people more information than they can handle. And because she can cut to the chase, providing voluminous information in a direct, nonjudgmental way, some people see Maria as abrupt or impersonal.

Concrete people like Keiko and Maria deal with the daily events of the world as facts that are likely to increase probabilities or possibilities. They think in terms of a beginning and an end. By contrast, abstract people like Cynthia and Jason function in terms of relationships with people or ideas. All four of these individuals can and do ask all of the Four *P* questions. But as with all human beings, they tend to focus on one of the questions more than the other three. Researchers don't know whether this preference is inherited or learned, but most lean toward a combination of the two.

Figure 1.5 illustrates the similarities and differences among Cynthia, Jason, Maria, and Keiko as I have described them in *The Real Colors Homeowner's Guide* (Johnson, 2004).

Let's shift our focus now to an examination of how the Four *P*s emerge within a public school environment.

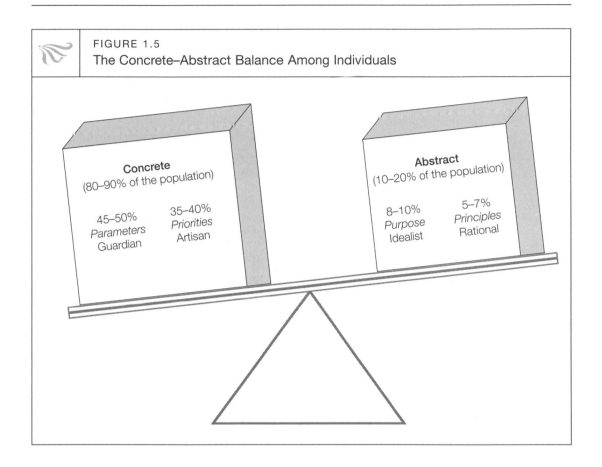

FIGURE 1.5

The Concrete–Abstract Balance Among Individuals

Concrete
(80–90% of the population)

45–50%
Parameters
Guardian

35–40%
Priorities
Artisan

Abstract
(10–20% of the population)

8–10%
Purpose
Idealist

5–7%
Principles
Rational

The Four *P*s and Organizations

Dave was an experienced high school principal whose staff was committed to a block schedule. When he asked his teachers to consider modifications to their schedule, the staff immediately opposed them. They insisted that "everyone knew" they could do more for students if they had more time—it was a *given*. "If we all agreed to this schedule just six years ago, why are we talking about changing it now?" they asked. "Besides, it works effectively for most of our students." Their opposition was so vehement, in fact, that Dave never got to the important question: "How are our actions at the school level meeting students' needs?"

The staff's response to Dave's suggestion shows how steeped in parameters educators are. They based their assumptions on past experiences. Myers and McCaulley (1985) indicate that somewhere between 65 and 70 percent of educators are likely to engage with their world from a parameters position—opting for ideas and experiences that are likely to bring about expected results (probability). The reactions of Dave's staff also focused on how scheduling changes might affect people. According to Myers and McCaulley, approximately 25 to 35 percent of educators connect with their world on the basis of human relationships.

When we add up the parameters and purpose percentages in a public school environment, we find that nearly 95 percent of educators approach learning from either perspective: why is this program or service important for students, and what are the rules for making decisions about these programs and services? Obviously, this preponderance leaves less than 10 percent of educators engaging with learning issues in terms of priorities or principles. These percentages lead to de facto profiling in public schools. Is it any wonder that educators spend more time defending programs than analyzing their effectiveness, or that change comes so slowly to the public schools? And is it any wonder that a gap exists between purpose and practice? Figure 1.6 illustrates the fact that analysis- and action-oriented stakeholders are in short supply in most school districts.

The neglect of these analysis and action considerations is not a matter of design. It is a factor of the personality of a school district environment. Most school districts give lip service to data-driven decision making, but they lack the voices in day-to-day planning and practice that speak for analysis and action. Without such voices, there is little incentive to ensure that these issues will be addressed in a careful, deliberate manner.

These statistics become even more disturbing when we consider which parents and community members are likely to engage in day-to-day activities within a public school. People who have been most successful in schools and

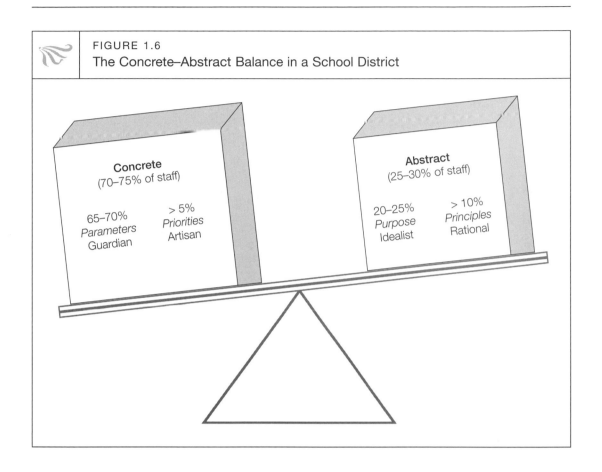

FIGURE 1.6

The Concrete–Abstract Balance in a School District

Concrete
(70–75% of staff)

65–70%
Parameters
Guardian

> 5%
Priorities
Artisan

Abstract
(25–30% of staff)

20–25%
Purpose
Idealist

> 10%
Principles
Rational

who have a natural tendency to assume responsibilities for the future of their community—purpose and parameters folks—tend to feel comfortable in a school setting. People tend to migrate toward those who share their values about learning and teaching. This fact increases the tendency to talk about differences but to conduct business as usual. It is human to want to stick with what we know—opting for probability as opposed to possibilities.

Given this reality, is it any wonder that many public school students lack experiences in critical thinking and problem solving? Is it any wonder that the general society remains divided about the effectiveness of our public schools? Is it any wonder that schools are slow to change? Our public schools are filled with good people who are doing what they do effectively. The question is, are the things that public schools do well preparing students for success in the real world?

Neither the closed world of "givens" nor its counterpart, "no guidelines whatsoever," fully addresses the needs of public school students. Quality schools provide a balance between discovery and exploration and between values and standards. We want students to learn basic skills and appreciate their culture. But they also need opportunities to think critically and creatively so that they can explore new and better solutions to real-life problems. We need a commitment to a common purpose rather than an adherence to personal agendas; an understanding of decision-making parameters rather than politics as usual; an adherence to principles that identify learning-teaching successes rather than a perpetual parade of programs and services; and an understanding that while perfection may not be possible, public school communities can leverage their resources toward priorities that promote success for *all* students.

Let's examine how leaders can manage a school organization in ways that allow people to achieve quality and to sustain it over time and across groups and communities.

Managing the Organization to Ensure Balance

Quality in public schools runs deeper than curriculum and instructional delivery: it goes to the very heart of our thinking about what students need to know and be able to do as a result of their school experience. To promote quality in any form, school leaders must seek what Quinn (1996) calls "deep change." Rather than managing people to fit the existing school culture, leaders need to manage the school culture to address various perspectives of quality. They need to ask stakeholders to describe what students, teachers, parents, administrators, and school board members would be doing in a quality school:

- How would they be interacting with one another?
- How would they be making decisions about when to move the target(s) for quality?
- How would they be holding one another accountable for success?
- How would they be allocating time and resources to achieve their goals?

Answers to these questions can help leaders paint a target for success, a common purpose for learning.

The secret to sustaining quality lies in stakeholders' ability to link purpose and practice. The organizational structures of the school district must encourage and support people to think about the following:

- The *purpose* of learning
- The *parameters* people use to decide what success looks like at any given time in any given setting
- The steps people follow to align daily classroom learning practices with organizational *principles*
- The *priorities* people establish to promote the greatest likelihood of success for all students

Leaders can encourage and support stakeholders as they ask all of the Four *P* questions, rather than relying on the one or two they have become accustomed to asking. Because parents and educators have formed habits of thinking that often fail to engage all areas of their Four *P* capabilities, school leaders must build the Four *P* questions into the very fabric of the change process.

Asking the Four *P* Questions from the Classroom to the Boardroom

Schools succeed when *all* children succeed, and quality is enhanced when stakeholders articulate what success looks like. School leaders can use the Four *P*s to paint a clear target for school improvement that includes multiple perspectives of success:

- *Purpose:* What do we believe students should know and be able to do as a result of their school experience? (Why is this important?)
- *Parameters:* Given these goals, how will we manage organizational structures to focus on appropriate progress for all students? (What are the rules of engagement?)
- *Principles:* Given these benchmarks, who is accountable for monitoring, adjusting, and aligning programs and services from the classroom to the boardroom? (How do we make this work?)
- *Priorities:* What evidence do we have that our programs and services can make a positive difference for student achievement and well-being now and in the future? (Will this make a difference?)

You can engage your stakeholders in this type of thinking through what Schön (1983) refers to as reflective planning—reflection on what students need to know and be able to do as a result of their school experiences. Reflection begins at the classroom and proceeds to the boardroom, where students' needs are translated into district goals. These district goals are then reframed within each level (elementary, middle, and high school) at each site, within each department/grade level, and within each classroom. Figure 1.7 illustrates how reflective planning works.

Reflective planning engages stakeholders in what Saban, Killion, and Green (1994) refer to as a centric process that moves from individuals to increasingly larger groups until it includes all the school district's stakeholder groups.

It is important for stakeholders to know what they believe and to recognize past successes in order to sustain quality schools. As a new superintendent, Jack worked with his school board, key staff, and community leaders to develop community forums where stakeholders could express their opinions about what was working well and what they thought could be done to make the district more effective. After the very first forum, differences emerged within and among groups. Rather than bringing people together, Jack's process seemed to pit staff against parents, with administrators and board members stuck in the middle.

FIGURE 1.7
Reflective Planning

Students' needs:

- As an individual, I believe the purpose of learning is . . .
- As a group (department, school site, grade level), we have reframed our individual beliefs about learning to include . . .
- As a total school community, we have reframed our groups' beliefs to include . . .

Goals for student learning:

- As a total school community, our goals will be to achieve . . .
- As a group (department, school site, grade level), we will reframe these goals to achieve . . .
- As an individual, I will reframe these goals at the classroom level to achieve . . .

Despite his good intentions, Jack had leaped beyond the purpose question to parameters questions: "How has our reframed purpose changed the rules of engagement? Who needs to be involved and in what capacities?" On the one hand, it is difficult to determine whether or not we are successful until we have described what success looks like. On the other hand, if we stop after having decided on a purpose, our change process will amount to little more than a dream of what might have been—another plan to gather dust on a shelf in the superintendent's office. To answer Jack's questions, stakeholders need to evaluate existing operating parameters in terms of their reframed purpose.

Deciding Who Should Answer the Four *P* Questions in Various Settings

If stakeholders are to close the gap between purpose and practice, they need to develop parameters for determining who makes what decisions. These parameters involve a backward mapping process: If kids are to be doing X in five years, what growth targets should we set for this year? What will teachers need to do to help students reach these targets? If teachers need to do X, what will administrators need to do to support them? If administrators do X, what will school board members need to do to support them? If the school district does X, what will the community need to do to support it?

This backward mapping requires people to make many decisions, from the classroom to the boardroom. These decisions, in turn, create a need for shared decision-making procedures that go beyond tacit understandings. Too frequently, decision-making processes are vague at best, if not totally non-existent. In such situations, even an experienced administrator can encounter problems aligning short-term decisions with long-term goals.

Tom, an experienced principal, took a new position in a school district that prided itself on shared decision making. Within his first week on the new job, he needed to hire three teachers. He discussed hiring procedures with the human resources director and with several of the district's most experienced principals, all of whom assured Tom that hiring decisions were site based and shared with staff and parents.

Tom's department chairs and members of the parent advisory committee, several of whom were also new to their positions, had varying opinions about how the process had been or should have been conducted in the past. With only the vaguest of written decision-making parameters—the call for teachers and parents to be involved in hiring decisions—Tom asked the department chairs and the chair of the advisory committee to help him organize an interview team. After agreeing on needs, position requirements, interview questions, and selection procedures, the committee recommended individuals to fill two positions but remained unalterably split on who should fill the third. Tom thanked the group for its help and said he would make the final decision on the third position after checking references.

Not only did Tom's decision annoy the interview team, it completely alienated his staff and the advisory committee. The staff and parents had failed to align their stated purpose for shared decision making with practical written procedures to make it work. The hiring task took on a life of its own, overshadowing district goals for student achievement and well-being.

Even when a school district has reframed its goals throughout the organization, it is important to evaluate which stakeholders need to be involved in various decisions at each level and how they will be involved. These decisions need to follow the same parameters from the classroom to the boardroom and back to the classroom. Imagine how much easier Tom's task would have been if decision-making parameters for hiring in his district and building had already been written.

School leaders need to follow up the purpose question—"Why is this important?"—with a parameters question: "Who should be involved in establishing and adjusting our focus at any point in time?" (i.e., "What are the rules of engagement?"). What they are asking at this point is, "How will we align our general sense of purpose through this general set of decision-making parameters so that we make realistic connections among students, teachers, parents, and all stakeholder groups from the classroom to the boardroom?"

Establishing Underlying Principles That Define Quality in Various Settings

The fundamental principles underlying quality schools should be consistent at every level of the district. The target for quality must be growth for all students. The underlying goal of growth across all student subgroups should guide stakeholders' analyses of programs and services in multiple settings: classroom, grade/department, building, level (elementary, middle, and high school), and district. Quality requires people to be accountable for achieving this goal from one task to another. Stakeholders should hold themselves accountable for ensuring success rather than relying on supervisors to make all of the decisions. In this way, stakeholders work *with* one another rather than *for* the district. They form partnerships.

When Dave, the experienced high school principal mentioned earlier, asked his teachers to consider modifications to their block schedule, he found himself at odds with his staff because he had failed to tie his process question back to the fundamental purpose of the block schedule. His first question should have been, "How is our block schedule meeting learners' needs?" Dave and his staff lost sight of the issue: how their daily block scheduling practices aligned with their stated purpose of meeting students' needs.

The staff was not the only source of resistance that Dave encountered. Many students and parents had also grown accustomed to the block schedule. By the time Dave shifted his focus to his parent and student advisory groups, they were already forming opinions on the basis of their informal conversations with teachers. Soon Dave told his superintendent that this investigation was not worth the price of student, staff, and parent stress. He thought this investigation could even become career-threatening for himself and for the superintendent.

Most school district mission statements refer to success for *all* students, not *most* students. Therefore, another fundamental question for Dave should have been, "For which students is our block schedule working, under what conditions, based on what evidence?" Dave needed to begin the investigation of block scheduling in a way that showed that he valued what his staff had already achieved, leaving them to suggest further improvements. Then he could have followed that discussion with a question about how to use these successes as a foundation for modifying the schedule to make programs and services accessible to more students.

Quality schools depend on individuals and groups holding themselves accountable for the effect of their actions on student achievement and well-being. Reflective planning requires stakeholders to align targets and tasks and to use student achievement data to measure the effectiveness of various implementation strategies. This is the process question: "How will I/we make this work?" Individuals and groups need to agree on what they are accountable for and to whom they are accountable. Accountability is a two-way process that identifies resource needs based on programs and services that work.

Establishing Organizational Priorities

The quality of a school district depends ultimately on individuals and groups asking, "Will what I am/we are doing make a difference?" This is a question of leveraging resources toward organizational priorities. Many programs and services work for some groups of students or are preferred by parents, teachers, and others; what school leaders need to know is which ones will give them the greatest leverage toward achieving success for *all* students.

In Dave's situation, students, parents, and staff were satisfied with the block schedule. But priorities should not be based on satisfaction alone. Satisfaction issues emerged because 25 to 30 percent of Dave's teachers were Idealists who valued positive relationships with their peers. They were also focused more on fairness and the nuts-and-bolts issues of scheduling than on student achievement and well-being. Staff members described their needs as more time, smaller classes, and more support from administrators, parents, and the community. These issues emerged because 60 to 70 percent of the teachers were Guardians who tended to focus on management—that is, parameters—issues.

Dave's foray into problem solving and data-driven decision making demonstrates that it is seldom easy to leverage resources when decisions require people to set aside personal comfort and management issues. It is never easy for educators and parents to make tough choices that call long-held assumptions about schools and learning into question. But if they have been involved in establishing the purpose, parameters, and processes that guide their work, they will have a deeper appreciation of the need for programs and services to be both effective and efficient. Priority decisions must be aligned with specific goals, targets, and quantifiable results. The process of setting priorities should begin with a review of successes and conclude with budget allocations.

You and your stakeholders can use the Four Ps to develop a common definition of quality rather than having it defined by philosophical or political agendas. You can help stakeholders use their individual and group strengths to create a balanced organizational personality for your district. You can sustain quality by shifting stakeholders' thinking from prioritizing goals to prioritizing programs and services. Programs and services should leverage progress toward the community's goals—from purpose to results.

Celebrating Differences

Stakeholders are more likely to develop a commitment to a change process when they have helped to create it. If school leaders encourage stakeholders to consider each of the Four Ps as a part of their daily practice, they can create a balance between organizational and individual needs. And when stakeholders share responsibilities for defining success, they begin to recognize that other personalities strengthen rather than detract from quality schools.

Leaders can create this celebration of differences by balancing individual and organizational personalities—by creating an organizational structure that addresses all of the Four *P* questions: purpose, parameters, principles, and priorities. This ongoing balance increases the likelihood of engaging the Idealist, Guardian, Rational, and Artisan perspectives so important to defining, achieving, and sustaining quality schools.

It is impossible for leaders to determine whether stakeholders are being beautifully and necessarily different or arbitrarily difficult. But by providing opportunities for all stakeholders to participate in the planning process, you can encourage them to use their differences in positive ways. In the Thompson School District and in several other districts around the country, I have introduced the Four *P*s as a reflective process that differs from typical planning approaches in two ways: (1) it models the learning process we want to create in the classroom, and (2) it links individual and organizational personalities to sustain change over time and across groups and communities.

Here is a Thompson School District example of how ongoing participation can lead to quality:

- More than 1,200 staff and community members participated in the planning process through meetings, luncheons with community leaders, and other means. The district's goals addressed the Four *P*s: purpose through a goal for safety and belonging, parameters through a goal for basic skills, principles through a goal for critical thinking and creativity, and priorities through a goal for school-to-life experiences. In addition, the plan outlined what stakeholders referred to as underlying principles that were important if not quite quantifiable.
- At quarterly luncheons with the superintendent over a three-year period, high school student government officers were able to list and discuss the district's goals and how they were involved in activities that supported the goals.

- Staff members from five middle schools and 18 elementary schools were able to identify programs and services that were most effective in achieving district goals.
- The district accountability advisory committee was able to clarify information that they needed to see as evidence of progress, and site administrators were able to develop rubrics for gathering and analyzing successes.
- The school board was able to focus budget allocations on data relative to each of the four school district goals.
- A high school program review process was developed to determine how the district's five high schools could have a common focus without losing the flexibility to address the unique needs of their students.
- Staff requested professional development that would focus on study groups aimed at specific ways to differentiate instruction for students. One such study group asked for additional time and resources to integrate critical thinking into daily classroom instruction.

The challenge for school leaders is getting stakeholders to think differently about change. Again, 65 to 70 percent of most school staffs are Guardians, as are many of the parents who serve on school advisory councils. Most of the remainder of staff and highly involved parents are Idealists—approximately 25 to 30 percent. With 90 to 95 percent of involved stakeholders focused on purpose and parameters, there is little natural inclination toward the Rational and Artisan aspects of the quality profile. Guardians and Idealists recognize the need for analysis and action, but they don't necessarily engage in them. They practice what works for their personality types—building positive relationships and a stable environment.

School leaders can't change stakeholders' personalities, but they can manage a school district's planning process to bring more stakeholders to the table—or to take the table to the stakeholders. A broader cross section of stakeholders at the planning table ensures a more inclusive definition of success that has broad stakeholder support. Leaders can use the Four *P*s to create a shared commitment to quality schools.

The next chapter shows how you can ask the right questions and listen to the intent behind people's responses. But before we consider these questions, take a moment to respond to the following school district personality inventory.

Conducting a School District Personality Inventory

Write out your answers to the following questions and discuss them with other stakeholders whose help you will need to make reframing effective.

1. To what extent do you analyze your leadership decisions in terms of the Four Ps? (List specific examples.)
2. To what extent do the management structures in your district promote reflective planning in terms of the Four Ps? (In other words, to what extent are you or other district leaders willing to share decision making with some or all stakeholders?)
3. What examples of the Four Ps do you see your stakeholders bringing to the planning table?
4. To what extent are stakeholders in your district truly open to possibilities rather than looking for support for their own ideas?
5. What would it take to introduce the Four Ps into your school or district?
6. What other projects or processes already under way in the district might interfere with or need to be coordinated with the introduction of reflective planning?
7. What is your district's history with change (depth, frequency, and effectiveness)?
8. How do you plan to introduce or expand the Four Ps in your school or district? (Be specific.)
9. How do you plan to apply the Four Ps to your management structures to provide for reflective planning? (Again, be specific.)

Asking Quality Questions

If you want to find out what people value, ask them. Their answers may surprise you.

Fifty angry citizens pack the boardroom. Half the group is made up of staff members, the rest of parents. They fidget and murmur, and then applaud as one person after another addresses the ills of the proposed middle school schedule. Their common purpose lies in what they don't want.

Judy, an experienced school board member, listens attentively as parents and staff describe the benefits of the status quo. She is intrigued by the group's conflicting views of quality. "If random acts of effectiveness are the closest we can come to critical thinking," Judy says, "we're in trouble."

Quality is not equivalent to luck, and requires more than success for a few. It is achieved when people connect random acts of effectiveness into consistent patterns of success across groups and communities. The first step toward creating quality schools is recognizing that stakeholders define quality in different ways. The second step is recognizing these differences as assets rather than obstacles.

In this chapter, you will learn how to ask questions that identify different aspects of success as seen from the perspectives of different personalities:

Idealist, Guardian, Rational, and Artisan. You can use these questions to build what I call a "connected learning community" (Johnson, 1999), described in Figure 2.1.

Lieberman and Grolnick (1997) suggest that a learning community has four fundamental characteristics: a commitment to a shared purpose, equal access to information, collaboration and reflection, and leadership and facilitation. You can use the Four *P* questions to develop relationships among your stakeholders so that they become a connected learning community. These questions help stakeholders develop a common definition of quality:

- *Purpose:* What should students know and be able to do as a result of their school experience?
- *Parameters:* What will staff need to know and be able to do in order to create programs and services that address students' needs?
- *Principles:* Who will monitor, align, and adjust programs and services so that all students are successful?

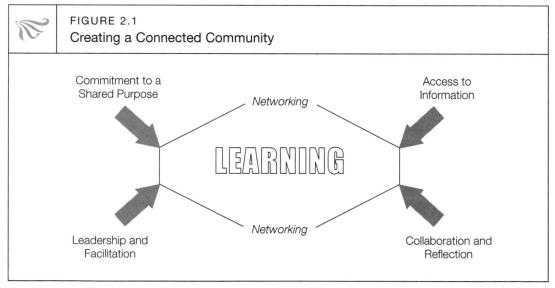

FIGURE 2.1
Creating a Connected Community

Source: Adapted from Johnson (1999).

- *Priorities:* How will the school board identify and support quality programs and services?

As their target shifts because of rising expectations, connected learning communities can revisit these questions to trace their progress over time.

In the previous chapter, we considered how to get various stakeholders to the table so that the school district's personality becomes more consistent with the personality of the larger community. But how can you create a culture that sustains that balance over time?

Purpose Questions

Effective schools develop a commitment to a shared purpose. This commitment runs deeper than spoken or written goals—it goes to the heart of the community culture. It is flexible because it is a matter of understanding rather than a matter of rules. For example, let's assume that your community's vision for success calls for improving reading achievement by 15 percent across the district within five years. In this case, schools and classrooms that begin with low reading achievement may need to establish a multiyear improvement plan, whereas those that are already at or near the goal may want to modify successful practices for underachieving student subgroups—different goals, same purpose.

When goals are achieved at any level of the organization, classroom teachers, departments, and schools need to decide where to go next. They need to adjust their target. Do they go for another 15 percent or, having achieved success as envisioned, do they hold onto those reading gains and focus their efforts in another direction? In such situations, reading is still a significant part of the district's purpose, but the target has been reframed to be appropriate across various buildings and classrooms. To paint a clear target for both short-term and long-term definitions of quality, you need to help stakeholders at all levels of the district ask other effective questions.

People usually structure questions and interpret answers from their own frame of reference. Hearing an answer to a "purpose" question, Idealists want to move on while everyone is in agreement, Guardians want to create rules and procedures that ensure consistent expectations among all stakeholders, Rationals want to create a process to monitor progress, and Artisans want to move directly to a solution. "The Four *P*s Listener's Guide" in Figure 2.2 illustrates how you can help Guardians, Rationals, and Artisans deal effectively with "purpose" questions.

To an Idealist, rules and procedures require people to do something as opposed to developing a natural commitment to a shared purpose. They believe that an answer to the "purpose" question is all you need to make schools more effective. But few stakeholders would argue with the necessity of answering the following questions:

- What evidence do we have that our programs and services actually make a difference for students?
- For which students or groups of students do they work?
- What are the conditions under which success occurs?
- Where do we go from here to ensure success for all students?

FIGURE 2.2

The Four *P*s Listener's Guide

Here are some ways to give responses to a "purpose" question a slight twist to keep the focus on quality.

Parameters Response to a Purpose Question	Principles Response to a Purpose Question	Priorities Response to a Purpose Question
From: "Okay, let's agree on the rules for . . ." To: "That might work, but can you tell us what it might look like in a classroom?"	From: "Then we will need a process to . . ." To: "I can see your point, but can we talk about how that might affect us in the following areas . . . ?"	From: "I don't think that is nearly as important as . . ." To: "That sounds exciting, but is this how we can get the biggest bang for our buck in this area?"

These questions shift the focus from *what we want* to *what is working* for various groups of students. While the answers may differ from one classroom, school, or level to another, they are aligned with a common target. Decisions made in one classroom do not compete with decisions made in other venues. Figure 2.3 provides an example of how the purpose question might be reframed across organizational structures.

Once school district goals have been established, the process is reversed: how can we *reframe* these goals at the elementary, middle, or high school level; at the building level; within each team or department; and within each classroom? A similar process is then followed for the evaluation, analysis, and leveraging questions. For example, given our goals, what will our performance target be for this classroom?

Thompson School District's four high schools were engaged in a program review to determine how they could sustain quality in the future. One high school's staff saw the review as an opportunity to create positive change. The other staffs complained that it ignored and even devalued past

---

FIGURE 2.3
Reframing Critical Questions

Classroom: How can we, at the classroom level, frame our common expectations for what students need to know and be able to do?

Department/Grade: How can we reframe those expectations so that they are consistent within our department/grade?

Building: Given different expectations across content areas, how can we reframe our expectations so that they are consistent within our building?

Elementary/Middle/High School Levels: Given what we know about students at this level, how can we reframe our expectations so that they are consistent across our level?

District: Given what we know about our community, how can we frame goals to provide direction across the district?

professional accomplishments. Many staff members believed that the review process was moving entirely too fast, whereas many community members wanted school leaders to move more quickly.

School leaders recognized these reactions as a natural part of the change process. Everyone wanted progress, but no one wanted to change. Acknowledging these differences, school leaders reassured both staff and parents that they recognized Thompson's rich history of success by repeating two questions over and over again: How can we gather evidence to identify which programs and services work best for various student subgroups? And how can we build on these success stories so that all students can be successful?

Questions automatically imply change, especially in an organization that is 65 to 70 percent Guardian. But questions can also determine how successful a change process will be. A school district's purpose defines its vision of quality. That purpose should become the standard against which stakeholders measure their daily practices. You can use questions like those in Figure 2.4 to clarify your stakeholders' vision of success; answers to these questions help stakeholders paint the quality target more clearly throughout the school district.

FIGURE 2.4
Purpose Questions to Clarify Definition of Success

Critical Question	Sample Response
What was the old standard?	Third grade students should demonstrate fluency while reading 25 words per minute.
What goal(s) was this standard designed to achieve?	Children should read to learn by the end of 3rd grade.
What examples of success do we have relative to this goal?	We have previous performance in our district and research from other schools.
How might existing goals and instructional strategies be limiting our interpretation of this data?	We used a balanced literacy approach that included . . .

Critical questions elevate the level of conversation. They shift the focus from a simple right or wrong to dimensions of success—success for whom, under what conditions, and given what evidence? Critical questions engage the community's collective energy toward improving student achievement and well-being rather than simply making programs work. This is not change for the sake of change—it is a carefully crafted set of parameters defined in terms of learning outcomes rather than instructional philosophies. Reflective questions eliminate the need for a bell curve, because their purpose is to make success accessible to all students.

Guardians tend to define quality in terms of the extent to which people have worked hard and have followed the rules. It is not difficult to demonstrate that people who follow the rules and practice (do their homework) do well in school. Approximately 50 percent of students are Guardians who see the world from the same perspective as their teachers see it (Keirsey & Bates, 1998). Unfortunately, this style of learning is not effective for all students.

A quick analysis of research conducted by Marzano, Pickering, and Pollock (2001) demonstrates that two Rational strategies—recognizing similarities and differences, and summarizing and note taking—are actually more significant in improving student performance than practicing homework. Figure 2.5 lists nine strategies and the percentile gains associated with their use. Can you find examples of the Four *P*s in this list?

Critical questions should focus on student needs and evolve from an expectation of success for all students. They should model the type of learning on the adult level that we want to encourage in our classrooms and schools. Because students' needs vary among schools and classrooms, instructional decisions require more than an agreed-upon set of decision-making parameters. They require questions that promote access to information and an understanding of different learning styles and modalities.

Access Questions

School reform efforts over the past 100 years have been little more than philosophical arguments between the two largest personality groups in our

FIGURE 2.5
Instructional Strategies and Student Performance

Strategy	Percentile Gains
Recognizing similarities and differences	45
Summarizing and note taking	37
Providing feedback that reinforces effort	29
Assigning homework and guided practice	28
Using nonlinguistic representations (pictures, graphs, demonstrations, etc.)	27
Engaging in cooperative learning	27
Stating objectives and getting feedback on results	23
Creating and testing hypotheses	23
Asking questions and providing cues and advanced organizers	22

Source: Summary of research reported in Marzano, Pickering, and Pollock (2001).

society—Guardians (45 to 50 percent of the population) and Artisans (35 to 40 percent). Idealists (15 to 20 percent) weigh in from time to time with enough influence to keep schools relatively pleasant places for most students and staff to work. The problem is not that adults do not care, but that it is difficult for adults to think beyond the learning strategy that works for them.

Do your schools make success accessible to all students or only to those who learn the way you teach? What are you willing to do for students whose needs are not being met? Rather than prioritizing one subject or teaching strategy over another, encourage your stakeholders to ask which programs and services meet the needs of which students—which programs work for whom, under what conditions, and given what evidence?

You can design critical questions that focus and coordinate the work of numerous stakeholders across your school district. The right critical questions can help stakeholders clarify when they need to adjust the quality target—turning decision making into a factor of students' needs rather than an element of adults' political or philosophical belief systems. Stakeholders need to set criteria to gauge when it is time to move the target rather than argue about who will decide when the target should be moved. One elementary school principal asked his site accountability advisory committee the following access questions:

- What future standard(s) will indicate that our students are reading to learn at the end of 3rd grade?
- What assessments will we use to determine the success of our strategies?
- How will we use the data in our ongoing planning efforts?
- Have we made information accessible to all stakeholders?
- How will we ensure that the people most directly affected by a change have an opportunity to express their perspectives before, during, and after implementation?
- Are we modeling critical thinking and creativity for our students through this process?
- What is our individual and collective accountability for results?

Think about how your stakeholders might respond to these access questions. Would they say, "Children should be able to read a passage from a nonfiction book with appropriate fluency and comprehension"? Might they say, "Aural learners will probably benefit from X, whereas bodily-kinesthetic and spatial learners may need Y"? Whatever their answers, their discussions would paint a clearer target. The discussions generated by reflective questions provide a common understanding among stakeholders: "Where should the target be placed now, and how will we decide when to move it at some date in the future?"

Having access to information involves far more than knowing *what* is going on—it includes knowing the *implications* of what is going on. Access questions help stakeholders think about the impact of their decisions on various groups of students and on various operational procedures. For example, in one Colorado school district, members of a site accountability advisory committee agreed to a general statement of purpose recommending special courses for non-English-speaking students. However, their agreement soon dissipated when they learned that these special courses jeopardized funding for other courses and required a longer school day. Course options accomplish very little unless they are accompanied by scheduling flexibility and other considerations.

Stakeholders need to understand how decisions made during the planning process are likely to affect daily operations. This information helps them

- Make connections among decisions in various venues,
- Clarify issues and state problems in manageable terms,
- Make better decisions about the types of information they need and where that information can be found,
- Think critically and creatively about problems and about the impact of potential solutions, and
- Understand their individual and collective accountability for results.

Leaders can build a vision for a school district with or without shared decision making. But can they sustain the vision over time? Enthusiasm sets a group in motion. Focusing and sustaining that momentum require stakeholders to ask critical questions about their responsibilities as learners and teachers.

Collaboration and Reflection Questions

The key to growth is not how much data a school district can amass but what stakeholders do once they have the data. Phye (1997) suggests four questions that should guide assessment discussions. How could you and your stakeholders use these questions to reflect on the data about achievement gains related to learning strategies mentioned earlier in Figure 2.5?

- Why is the assessment necessary?
- What forms of assessment are most appropriate given this purpose?
- What will we do with the assessment information once it has been collected?
- How will the assessment information be reported and stored in ways that benefit students and respect individual privacy rights?

To address those four questions, the assistant superintendent in Glenview, Illinois, asked his district's stakeholders to implement the following processes:

- Identify personal expectations for schools and learning
- Compare expectations in a group setting
- Ask open-ended questions that clarify conflicting expectations
- *Listen to* one another's answers rather than *listening for* the answers you expect
- Make decisions based on what you want to know about student progress rather than on what you need to prove

Marzano (2003) suggests that school leaders take three steps to make the most of student assessment:

- Implement an assessment system that provides timely feedback on specific knowledge and skills for specific students.
- Establish specific, challenging achievement goals for the school as a whole.
- Set specific goals for individual students.

An effective assessment system goes beyond test results. It establishes a set of underlying principles that connect individual assessments into an overall picture of growth for individual students, individual schools, and the entire school district. Thompson School District's strategic plan includes four goal areas: basic skills, critical thinking and creativity, safety and belonging, and school-to-life skills. But the plan also includes a set of underlying principles that further refine people's definition of quality. Thompson stakeholders use the underlying principles listed in Figure 2.6 as a framework for developing data analysis questions.

In the following sections, I will illustrate how Thompson stakeholders have combined these underlying principles with Phye's four assessment questions to shape an effective accountability process.

Why Is the Assessment Necessary?

The mantra for sustaining quality should be "Find success and replicate it." A focus on success creates a positive, safe environment for accountability. School district stakeholders can use assessment data to identify discrepancies

---

FIGURE 2.6
Thompson School District's Underlying Principles of Learning

We believe that

- Education requires attention to the **whole child** (academic, physical, social, emotional, and ethical).
- Individuals develop a positive attitude toward learning and toward themselves as learners when their environment provides meaningful **opportunities for success.**
- All stakeholders are **accountable** and **share responsibility** for learning by initiating, keeping, and answering for personal commitments.
- **Communication** is everyone's responsibility.
- Students should learn and adults should demonstrate **respect** for themselves, for others, for property, and for individual and group differences.
- Learning is most effective when all stakeholders are **meaningfully involved** and have **high expectations** for themselves and others.
- A supportive learning environment requires **consistent expectations** for student performance within grades and **continuous progress in** preK–12.
- **Technology** should be **integrated** into the curriculum as a tool to meet **diverse learner needs.**

in student performance related to the whole child, including his or her academic, physical, social, emotional, and ethical growth. They can also

- Ask questions about opportunities for success by comparing achievement data by ethnicity, gender, disability, and limited English proficiency;
- Consider how they have been accountable for learning by identifying which programs and services correlate with success—success for whom, under what circumstances, and given what evidence; and
- Conduct action research to compare the effects of technology in a lab situation with a more integrated approach in a classroom setting.

These questions take accountability beyond issues of compliance to issues of quality. How are we meeting our responsibilities to one another, and how can we use this information to improve student achievement and well-being?

Figure 2.7 suggests how stakeholders can collect, analyze, and apply assessment data in ways that address those quality factors. The analysis of

---

FIGURE 2.7
Collaboration and Reflection Questions

To sustain quality, school leaders should build an accountability process that

- Establishes community priorities for student growth on a yearly basis;
- Evaluates programs and services in terms of district priorities;
- Identifies how students perform relative to state, national, and international standards;
- Develops instructional strategies that address various learning styles and modalities;
- Creates professional development activities that enhance the staff's ability to meet the needs of all students;
- Uses assessment data to refine and adjust daily practice consistent with the district's strategic goals; and
- Commits the school board to managing the district so that all schools meet district standards over time and across student subgroups.

student performance should indicate the number and percentage of all students attaining and exceeding the district's performance standards, as well as identify significant patterns of growth, low achievement, or achievement discrepancies. In addition, the plan should provide for the assessment of organizational achievement in terms of all district goals.

When the Thompson School Board adopted its strategic plan, one board member suggested it might be impractical to expect schools to assess their safety and belonging and other nonacademic goals. However, administrators were not willing to hold themselves or their staff accountable for goals that could not be assessed. To solve this conundrum, the staff developed a definition of safety and belonging, examples of what a safe and inclusive environment might look like, and methods for collecting data on the extent to which students felt a sense of safety and belonging at school. The essential components of the definition are listed in Figure 2.8.

Once the definition and accompanying examples were developed, it was possible for staff to determine what evidence could be gathered from existing sources and what additional assessments needed to be developed. Existing data sources included discipline referrals, suspension rates, and

---

FIGURE 2.8
Thompson School District's Definition of Safety and Belonging

Personal Safety: physical and emotional

Acceptance and Tolerance: student-to-student and adult-to-student relationships

Opportunity for Academic Success: curriculum adaptations, instructional adaptations, and alternative schedules

Self-Discipline and Personal Responsibility: individual choice and the acceptance of consequences that arise from such a decision

Resiliency and Empowerment: coping with the limits and consequences of life

attendance rates. One example of needed refinements was the revision of an existing satisfaction survey to coordinate questions with the five components in Figure 2.8.

The staff also collected input from students and parents through informal conversations, student newspaper articles, superintendent luncheons with student government officers and community leaders, and so on. The district accountability advisory committee (DAAC) then asked administrators to provide information regarding the types of programs and services available to students, the number of people accessing them, and their correlation with successful safety results.

What Forms of Assessment Are Most Appropriate Given This Purpose?

Danielson (2002) suggests the following four steps for designing assessments:

- Arriving at consensus on the content of the assessment
- Determining appropriate methodology for the assessment
- Developing assessment rubrics
- Setting performance benchmarks

School leaders can use the adaptation of Danielson's Rubric for Assessment shown in Figure 2.9 to guide stakeholders' reflections on their own accountability process.

What Will Be Done with the Assessment Information Once It Has Been Collected?

In terms of the Thompson safety and belonging assessments, the DAAC requested that a baseline be established for all data sources so that progress could be analyzed over time. The DAAC also asked that school staffs begin to include assessment data as a part of their goal setting within the building action plans, and that the data be analyzed in terms of successful programs

FIGURE 2.9
Analyzing the Assessment Process

	Poor	Basic	Exemplary
Alignment with Goals	Assessment tools align with goals but lack consistency.	Common aligned tools exist at each site.	All schools use common aligned tools across groups and levels.
Methodologies	Assessment methodologies are limited.	Methodologies are varied according to goals.	Methodologies vary according to goals but are consistent across groups and levels.
Criteria and Standards	Standards are unclear and have not been shared with stakeholders.	Standards are clear within stakeholder groups but inconsistent across groups.	Standards are consistently defined and applied across stakeholder groups.
Interpretation and Reporting	Stakeholders interpret assessment data in a highly idiosyncratic manner, making it difficult to draw conclusions or coordinate responses.	Stakeholders use the assessment data to set individual and group goals at each school.	Stakeholders use the assessment data to set individual and group goals consistently across groups and levels.

Source: Adapted from Danielson (2002).

and strategies that could be shared across classrooms, buildings, and levels. Requests of this nature shifted the quality target to a higher level.

How Will the Assessment Information Be Reported and Stored in Ways That Benefit Students and Respect Individual Privacy Rights?

Demonstrating accountability is more involved than implementing a series of tests, but it's likely that your school district does not need to develop new or more complicated procedures to collect data regarding nonacademic goals. Let's use the Thompson safety and belonging example to demonstrate how you may already be collecting such information.

When the DAAC concluded that the validity and reliability of safety and belonging data gathering needed to be improved, district office staff focused on data that they were already collecting to comply with the 1994 Safe and Drug-Free Schools Act. District office staff asked principals to review their data and then met with them to discuss ways to improve their discipline procedures in accordance with the law. In the first year, student expulsions were cut almost in half. Of equal significance, in the middle school with the highest percentage of at-risk students, not one parent appealed a suspension or other disciplinary action to the district office.

This example illustrates that an effective student assessment program can be developed for both academic and nonacademic goals. The critical characteristics of such programs are outlined in Figure 2.10.

Leadership and Facilitation Questions

A simple list of educational successes will not be enough to convince your community that it needs to invest more money or time in public schools. Most staff and community members are not aware that 75 percent or more of

FIGURE 2.10
Thompson School District's Characteristics of Effective Assessments

Effective assessments

- Ask all stakeholders to reflect on the same data.
- Ask questions that move stakeholders from thinking about the data to acting on the data—goal setting, implementing a plan, data analysis, etc.
- Provide "early warning" features that allow problems to be diagnosed promptly so that students, teachers, and parents know what extra effort is necessary.
- Supply reliable and valid information on student and school performance that is reported to educators, parents, and the community.
- Create timely, practical reporting to enhance the use of data for student achievement, professional development, and curriculum improvement.

taxpayers around the country today do not have school-age children (Hodgkinson, 2003). This does not mean that these individuals do not care about education, but rather that schools are not necessarily high on their priority list. They value education, but they face other demands that have a more immediate effect on their day-to-day lives.

Leadership requires more than reporting information. It requires an ability to do so in a manner that is meaningful to different stakeholder groups throughout the community. When data do not support what we already "know," we tend to search for flaws in the system and in our leaders, and want to form new committees representing all stakeholder groups to "sort things out" and "improve communications." This is why it is so important for stakeholders to help school leaders report district successes to various community groups. You can often communicate more effectively by putting information in the hands of staff and parents so that they can share it with other members of the community.

Most stakeholders express a desire to analyze programs and services systematically. But test scores and other quantifiable data communicate only results; it's credible people who communicate values. People attend to those things that have a direct and compelling impact on their lives. For everything else, they trust the people they know to tell them what is really going on.

History demonstrates that it is possible to gain a political majority for numerous change proposals (Tyack & Cuban, 1995). However, when you have a narrow support base for a proposed change, you drastically decrease its life expectancy. Likewise, the commitment to a change that is implemented as a response to fear and chaos without the benefit of analysis and reflection time is likely to wane when a sense of safety and order returns. As Bruner and Bornstein (1989) suggest, people need time to live with and reflect on a newly attained skill before they can apply it or pass it on.

The public, particularly individuals who do not have children in school, expects school leaders to report on and support existing programs. To make these taxpayers more aware of school district needs, leaders need to get information into the hands of parents, teachers, and staff. If these individuals believe in the direction the school district is taking, they can assure the public that what students learn in school significantly improves their likelihood of becoming successful citizens and employees. Nonparent taxpayers want graduates who will contribute to the quality of life within their community. To promote this level of communication and support, you and your school board can ask the questions listed in Figure 2.11.

In 1995, Glenview students and staff participated with 19 other suburban Chicago school districts in the Third International Mathematics and Science Study. Following the study, Glenview teachers wanted to establish a planning day at the end of each quarter during which teachers could review results of their teaching practices in terms of their long-range district goals. This request conflicted with parents' expectations regarding the length of the school year.

During a year of monthly meetings, a cross section of stakeholders studied research regarding the following questions:

- Given our strategic plan goals and the diversity of our learners, how can we differentiate curriculum and instruction in ways that meet all students' needs?
- What skills does our staff have relative to differentiation?

FIGURE 2.11
Funding Priorities Questions That Attract Nonparent Taxpayers

- Do all employees and key committee members support our strategic goals?
- Do stakeholders understand how district needs, including mission-critical capital replacement and preventive maintenance needs, compete for a finite set of district resources?
- Do we have evidence of success beyond traditional assessments?
- Can we explain how our budget decisions support our strategic goals?
- Do we communicate a commitment to making our community a desirable place to live and raise a family?

- What additional skills will they need?
- How will we provide time for them to engage in professional development?

Following this year of research, one parent said to the Glenview school board, "You folks have all been at these monthly meetings. You have read the research and heard the discussions. Like me, many of you expected a big debate here tonight. In fact, after all I've said in the past about shortening the school year, I can't believe I'm saying this. But we all know what we need to do. Our kids need different kinds of instruction to be successful. And our teachers need time to look at student achievement data and plan for different learners. They need time for professional development. Vote 'yes' on these extra days, and let's get on with it."

Applause followed, and the school board voted unanimously to add four days to the school calendar for professional development. These stakeholders had been given a firsthand opportunity to understand the need for change.

Thompson School District involved more than 1,200 community members and staff directly in their goal-setting process. Then they used a legally required year-end report, monthly luncheons with business and community leaders, guest editorials in the local newspaper, and an electronic newsletter to communicate their successes.

If stakeholders, particularly those who do not have school-age children, are going to support quality schools, teachers and parents need to assure them that their dollars are not being wasted on the latest fads. These citizens want answers to the following questions:

- How effectively have the schools spent existing resources?
- Do school leaders know what students need to be successful in the "real world"?
- How can I know that my tax dollars are being leveraged to benefit students?
- Do the schools demonstrate the qualities that I value?

- Does the school staff appreciate and communicate effectively with the community?

Priorities announce to stakeholders that their work to this point has been meaningful and that they can, in fact, influence change in their school district over time and across subgroups. The school district's budget provides evidence that the school board is committed to supporting and sustaining quality. It is the most public demonstration to Artisans (the 35 to 40 percent of the public who demand action) that schools can act effectively and efficiently. You can use the questions in Figure 2.12 to help your stakeholders clarify your priorities.

There are numerous ways to make a funding plan work, each with its own set of advantages and disadvantages. However, to gain widespread support, plans for future spending must provide realistic options. Csikszentmihalyi (1990) suggests that people are most likely to feel a sense of success

---

FIGURE 2.12
Finding Success and Replicating It

To engage stakeholders in developing funding priorities, ask the following questions:

- What programs and services are you most proud of?
- Would you be willing to share your success stories with others?
- What evidence do you have that these success stories are real?
- What are the commonalities among success stories within your building or level?
- How could the district office support further development of these successes and encourage application of key principles to other program and service areas?

After summarizing information from these sessions, follow up with these questions:

- Did we accurately capture your successes?
- Now that we have discussed successes across your level (elementary, middle, or high school), which programs and services would you ask the school board to protect or expand?

(what he calls "flow") when their attention is invested in realistic goals and their skills match their opportunities for action. Flow requires feedback—feedback that is meaningful in terms of both the group purpose and the numerous individual definitions of purpose.

The format for success-sharing meetings needs to be simple and informal, but also celebratory. Have your flip charts and other materials ready, review your process several times for clarity, and make certain to verify your summary of the meeting with as many participants as possible. It is hard to establish a long-term projection of revenues and expenditures, but it is possible to establish ongoing procedures for the yearly consideration of prebudget issues consistent with the rationale, purpose, goals, and criteria outlined above.

Thompson principals used input from staff and site advisory committees to develop funding priority recommendations. A district leadership team reviewed this input for presentation to the DAAC; the superintendent then prepared budget recommendations based on this process. The leadership team identified needs within each division: student achievement, business services, human resources, and operational services. The process concluded with the school board commitments listed in Figure 2.13.

Adjusting the Target

Quality schools depend on stakeholders' ability to ask the right questions and to adjust their target for student achievement and well-being on an ongoing basis. Critical questions focus people's attention in order to make their tasks more manageable, and help them gain a better sense of the target at any given point in time. The following examples illustrate what can happen when people learn to ask the right questions and listen more carefully to one another's answers:

- The Clear Creek School District in Idaho Springs, Colorado, won an award from the National Council of States on Inservice Education for a staff development process based on key elements of the Four Ps.

FIGURE 2.13

Thompson School Board's Funding Commitments

1. The Board will base funding decisions on the extent to which they provide the greatest leverage toward achieving our strategic goals for all students.

2. We will achieve our common purpose through agreed-upon parameters, a persistent search for solutions, and a commitment to continuous progress.

3. We will educate, through high school, children who only a few years ago would have dropped out of school to enter the workforce.

4. We will partner with parents and the community to meet the demands of our technological world, changes in family structure and lifestyle, and an increasingly mobile population.

5. We will use technology to improve learning and manage information, but it is highly unlikely that technology will significantly decrease staff needs during the next 10 years.

6. We will work to meet new service demands within existing resources.

7. To gain the trust and support of our taxpayers, we will demonstrate that we can educate reliable workers and good citizens.

8. Our financial decisions will be based on a clear statement of purpose, a defined target, a plan for implementation, and a method for monitoring and evaluating (i.e., accountability) purposes.

9. While we accept the need to dream of possibilities, we expect a reasonable probability of success as a prerequisite to funding a project.

- The First in the World Consortium, from the Chicago suburbs, received support from the U.S. Department of Education for its staff development process based on aspects of the Four *P*s.
- When the Thompson school board used the Four *P*s in its budgeting process, three projects (including one that had existed for five years) were discontinued because of insufficient evidence that they improved student achievement and well-being.
- Two first-year programs for at-risk students that were formerly funded by grants were funded within the school district budget because more than 95 percent of the students served were in school and passing all courses.

- The Thompson school board and the teachers' association agreed to formulate proposals in the form of critical questions to reinforce problem solving in negotiations.
- Administrative and school board study session agendas focused on answering critical questions to focus conversations and ensure appropriate closure.
- In five feeder system meetings, only two individuals answered the question "What support do you need from the district office to continue your success?" in terms of smaller class size or more individual planning time. Teachers asked to continue book study groups, team time for studying and analyzing reading and mathematics strategies, and professional development for interdisciplinary planning.

You can move your planning process beyond the question "What school district programs are working and what programs need improvement?" by challenging your stakeholders to ask, "What do we believe students need to know and be able to do as a result of their school experience?" Then ask them, "Given our existing training and talent in these areas, what professional development opportunities will help us achieve these ends?"

You cannot change people's personalities, but you can use key questions to help them focus their thinking. Questions focused on the Four *P*s promote balanced planning that addresses a broad base of expectations for student success. When community members and staff see their ideas in action and see students meeting their expectations for learning, they stay focused on the target and are willing to move it as needed.

To be effective, your stakeholders need to make a habit of asking the Four *P* questions. In the next chapter, we will examine four districtwide protocols that you can use to make the Four *P* questions a habit in your school district. But before moving to these protocols, take a moment to consider what questions you and your stakeholders are currently asking.

1. To what extent do you currently use critical questions to change the way your stakeholders think about change?

2. How well do your questions address the Four *P*s? (List one or two questions under each of the Four *P*s that you have recently asked your stakeholders to consider.)

   Purpose:

   Parameters:

   Principles:

   Priorities:

3. To what extent do stakeholders in your school or district plan for continuous growth based on identifying past successes?

   a. Do you have procedures for collecting data on student assessment and well-being?

   b. What opportunities do you provide for various stakeholder groups to share ideas and plan together?

   c. Do you promote an environment that encourages stakeholders to ask questions and take reasonable risks to promote student achievement and well-being?

4. What is your preparation and implementation plan for asking better questions as follows?

   Step 1. Introduce or expand the Four *P* questions in your school or district.

   Step 2. Use the Four *P* questions to plan for a specific project or process.

   Step 3. Evaluate how well your Four *P* questions have shaped positive relationships among adults and positive outcomes for students.

5. What is your time line for the development and implementation processes?

3

Making Quality a Habit

A school district that cannot learn cannot teach.

People expect public schools to keep pace with change; they just don't want the schools themselves to change. Even when society moves the target outside the existing playing field, people forget to change the rules of the game inside the school walls.

As illustrated in Figure 3.1, quality schools meet community expectations. They match their stated purpose (left of the triangle) with their daily practice (right of the triangle). In quality public schools, the focus is on students and learning. Students' needs drive district goals (left). District goals then drive stakeholders' daily practices (right).

For quality to be sustained over time and across groups, stakeholders need to align their stated goals with their daily practices. The flow should run from needs identified at the classroom level to goals identified at the district level. Strategies emerging from the classroom level should be supported and analyzed by the district, and results reported across all levels so that stakeholders can adjust their targets to keep pace with changing expectations.

In the Glenview, Illinois, school district discussed in Chapter 2, the staff was asked to differentiate instruction for an increasingly diverse student

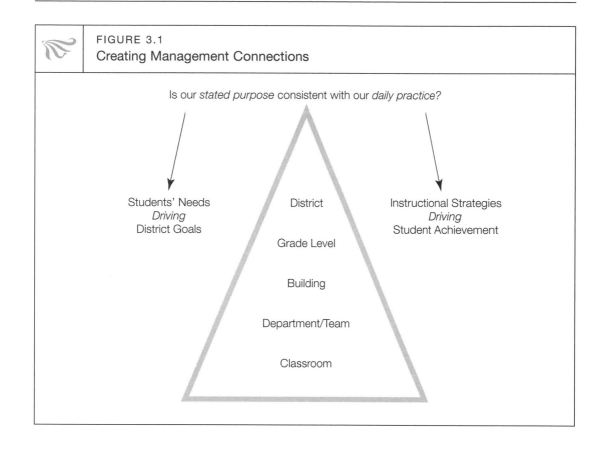

FIGURE 3.1
Creating Management Connections

Is our *stated purpose* consistent with our *daily practice?*

Students' Needs
Driving
District Goals

District

Grade Level

Building

Department/Team

Classroom

Instructional Strategies
Driving
Student Achievement

population. The Glenview staff had always met diverse student needs. Their students came from highly mobile families at Glenview Naval Air Station and from highly educated families of the bedroom communities of Chicago. But the influx of families who spoke English as a second language in the 1990s— which ranged from educated families from the former Soviet Union to poor Mexican families whose children had never before attended school—changed the rules of the game.

This situation called on the Glenview district to make choices about its honesty and integrity. According to Bennis (1989), honesty comes from setting a goal and trying to follow it ("walking the talk"). Integrity comes from being honest about what you are actually doing ("talking the walk"). The Glenview schools maintained their honesty by trying to uphold their pre-1990s expectations. But they lacked integrity, because their daily practices could not keep pace with their stated purpose. As most school communities do, Glenview tried to meet new societal expectations on top of existing expectations and within existing organizational parameters.

The Glenview community had learned to ask the right questions, such as "What do students need to know and be able to do?" But the schools were unable to escape old educational habits. Though they recognized that the rules of the game had changed, they failed to change their strategies to keep pace with those changes. When students' needs changed, district goals for student achievement remained artificially high. Consequently, even the best strategies were destined to fall short of expectations.

It is not enough to ask the right questions if you will not respond appropriately to the results of your investigations. You can help your district stakeholders learn to make data-driven decisions, but often that requires them to develop a whole new set of skills. According to Lieberman and Grolnick (1997), effective learning communities (those that can sustain meaningful change) demonstrate the following characteristics:

- Commitment to a common purpose
- Equal access to information
- Collaboration and reflection
- Leadership and facilitation

You and your stakeholders probably use some form of strategic planning to answer the question, "What do students need to know and be able to do as a result of their school experiences?" You have probably established either formal or informal decision-making parameters to answer the question "How can we manage programs and services so that all students show continuous progress across all content areas and grade levels?" But have you transformed your strategic goals into guiding *principles?* Have you established a process for setting *priorities* to match your daily practices with your stated purpose for learning?

The Four *Ps* and Expectations Within a Learning Community

Guardians are not comfortable when something they value does not work. Idealists are not comfortable when the people around them are unhappy. Together, these two groups compose 85 to 90 percent of the active stakeholders in most school districts. These stakeholders have developed habits that have worked for them in the past, but they must let go of these habits in order to develop an effective response to a new set of societal expectations.

This chapter describes how you can develop districtwide protocols that help your stakeholders create habits that promote an ongoing community of learners committed to quality schools regardless of shifts in community expectations. Figure 3.2 lists the Four *P* questions and the protocols that you can use to promote Four *P* habits in your school district.

Because 85 to 90 percent of your stakeholders are probably Guardians or Idealists, they have already mastered two of the Four *P* habits: purpose and parameters. Your challenge will be to get them to balance those habits with the *principles* and *priorities* habits. Your stakeholders need to become more comfortable with the questions "What do we need to know and be able to do in order to meet students' needs?" and "How will we identify and support programs and services that work?"

Do not make assumptions about the existing management structures in your school district. Even though you probably have a strategic plan and some understanding about how instructional decisions are made, your stakeholders have developed certain methods or expectations for dealing with day-to-day problems. As you read the next several pages, ask yourself what you will need to do to help your stakeholders form new habits that connect your daily practices with your stated purpose for learning.

FIGURE 3.2 Habit-Forming Protocols	
Critical Question	**Habit-Forming Protocol**
Purpose: What should students know and be able to do as a result of their school experience?	Strategic planning
Parameters: What do we need to know and be able to do in order to create programs and services that address students' needs?	Shared decision making
Principles: How will we monitor, align, and adjust programs and services so that all students are successful?	Accountability process
Priorities: How will we identify and support programs and services that work?	Funding priorities plan

Planning for a Shared Purpose

Agreeing to the wording of a goal is different from developing a commitment to a shared purpose. When stakeholders share a common purpose, they agree on what their goals should look like in action—that is, they agree on the target.

The first step in moving people toward a common purpose is to recognize all four faces of quality. Only 10 to 15 percent of the general population (and perhaps slightly more inside the school walls) views commitment to a shared purpose as a primary entry point to the world. These Idealists are often accused of "wearing rose-colored glasses"; people appreciate their good intentions but criticize them for their lack of follow-through.

Forty-five to 50 percent of the general population (and 65 to 70 percent of those in schools) views purpose as a result of hard work and playing by the rules. These Guardians believe that practice makes perfect and think that there would be plenty of time for creativity if people would work together to accomplish the "necessary" tasks first. They insist that basic skills (parameters) are a prerequisite to problem solving. They want to keep things simple.

Another 35 to 40 percent of people—although fewer than 5 percent in schools—believe that the route to quality lies in action. These Artisans believe that doing something is better than doing nothing at all. They become frustrated with the slow pace of change in the public schools. They want to identify what works (i.e., priorities) and get on with it.

Fewer than 5 percent of your stakeholders (inside and outside the school walls) are Rationals. This is the percentage of stakeholders whom you can expect to see a direct connection between the strategic plan and day-to-day activities in schools and classrooms. Rationals abhor the lack of systematic problem solving in public schools. They watch program after program being implemented with little or no planning and no criteria for analyzing results. They complain that most school communities make politics, rather than problem solving, the guiding principle for their actions.

If critical analysis and problem-solving skills are rare in all walks of life, why do school leaders spend so much time developing strategic plans? If so few Artisans get involved with the public schools as employees or participating consumers, why do school districts always seem to be involved in change? The answer is not that these stakeholders don't appreciate planning and risk taking, or that they lack the skills necessary to analyze and implement effective programs and services. It is that they simply have not developed planning and risk-taking habits. In the midst of daily activities, people lose sight of their intended purpose. These are deeply caring, hard-working people who spend so much time focusing on student learning and classroom management needs that they haven't developed problem-solving and risk-taking skills enough for them to become automatic (i.e., habits).

Laura, a high school math teacher, expresses it this way: "We all have such great ideas. Who is to say that one is better than another? Don't you think teachers do a better job when they are teaching what they enjoy? After all, teachers have unique styles too. Parents and administrators need to trust us."

There is nothing inherently wrong with Laura's position. In fact, when she stated her views at a site accountability advisory committee (SAAC) meeting, most parents agreed with her. One mother even asked why the district administration hadn't been more supportive of teachers. "What can we do," she wondered aloud, "to create more parent support for teachers?"

"It's always the same people at our SAAC meetings," another parent chimed in. "I wish we could require parents to attend at least three SAAC meetings each year. Quality schools don't just happen. They require a lot of hard work."

"Wait a minute; let's not be too critical of our parents," pleaded Molly, a 9th grade English teacher. "As a single parent myself, I know how difficult it can be to get home, fix dinner for the kids, pick up the sitter, and get back to the SAAC meeting by seven o'clock. We need to reach out to these parents. Isn't that what our safety and belonging goal is all about?"

"Why doesn't the school district hire social workers to work with some of our more needy families?" asked Bob, a veteran science teacher. "When we had social workers in the district, we had fewer discipline problems and more parent involvement. We had time to teach. Our kids deserve better. All we talk about anymore are test scores and the budget. We try to reach out to these kids, but there are only so many hours in a day. I move that we ask the district for more money for social workers."

Guardian teachers find support from one another and from Guardian parents. To Guardians, the "problem" lies with those parents who simply don't care—the ones who refuse to "work hard" at parenting. How can we think about effective teaching strategies until parents are willing to do their part? As Guardians see it, when strategy X does not yield result Y, someone has failed to work hard enough to achieve strategy X. They think we need to devote more time, money, and effort toward improving our implementation of strategy X, and feel we should not put money into new programs until we learn to use existing programs effectively. Occasionally, an Idealist like Molly reminds these Guardians that most parents are good people; some just need more support than others.

Bridges (1991) warns school leaders not to be surprised by stakeholders' resistance to change. You should expect and accept the signs of grieving and expect to give people information again and again. But unless you are committed to helping stakeholders play a significant role in each phase of the change process—from development and implementation to assessment and refinement—they will not commit to a shared purpose.

People need ways to break down long-term goals for change into manageable parts. You can help stakeholders by relating long-term strategies to connected short-term tasks, as illustrated in the Thompson School District responsibility matrix (Figure 3.3).

A single goal involves numerous tasks that need to be performed by numerous stakeholders. When people first see the responsibility matrix, they are overwhelmed by the complexity of the tasks and often realize that they must limit their scope. This pre-implementation pruning forces people to home in on realistic tasks—those that will help them match their goals with existing student needs, giving them the "biggest bang for the buck." As they consider who will be responsible to whom for what product, they come to appreciate the importance of cooperation and communication, and to appreciate differences as assets rather than roadblocks. The matrix clarifies who should coordinate and participate in each task as well as who needs to be informed of results. It also lists products and time lines.

The responsibility matrix has something for everyone: the goals appeal to Idealists by communicating a sense of *purpose,* the responsibilities appeal to the Guardians' need for manageable *parameters,* the logical sequence (*principles*) of tasks appeals to Rationals, and the listing of products and time lines (*priorities*) appeals to Artisans, who are happy that something is actually going to happen at last.

The matrix creates a scaffold for Guardians and Idealists to use as they review and refine their strategic plan. It paints a clear target for change and helps stakeholders understand how they can adjust the target from one year to the next. At the same time, the matrix builds connections between Idealist/ Guardian insiders and Rational/Artisan outsiders by outlining standards, specifying accountable participants and their audience, and identifying intended products and time lines.

FIGURE 3.3
Thompson School District's Strategic Planning Responsibility Matrix

Goal: To improve student achievement in reading and writing so that all student subgroups perform at least 10 percent above the state average.

Task	District Coordination	Site Facilitator	Leadership	Participation	Products	Audience	Time Lines
Language arts curriculum revision	Curriculum Improvement Council (CIC)	Director of curriculum, standards, articulation	Principal	Input from all stakeholder groups; recommendation by CIC to superintendent with final board approval	Curriculum revisions, assessments, curriculum materials	Students, parents, staff, community	Sept.–Jan. Conduct research and discussion

Feb.–March Draft recommendation and feedback

April–May Select materials

June–July Make recommendation to board; seek public discussion and approval

(Regular updates made available throughout process) |

The responsibility matrix brings life to the strategic plan at a district level. But the district purpose must be translated to buildings, departments and teams, and classrooms. You can use the school effectiveness plan illustrated in Figure 3.4 to make certain that students, parents, and staff have a clear understanding of what the district purpose looks like in their venue. This target helps stakeholders manage their own efforts and coordinate them with the efforts of other stakeholders throughout the school district.

The school effectiveness plan asks teachers and parents to think about what the district goals look like at their level:

- How are our students currently performing relative to district goals?
- What would be realistic targets for our students this year?
- What would our school look like if students were meeting these targets? What would teachers and students be doing, and how would parents and community members be involved?

You can use these questions to stimulate reflection among your stakeholders—first on an individual basis, then on a group basis (department,

---

FIGURE 3.4
School Effectiveness Plan

Task	Coordinator	Participation	Process/ Product	Communication/ Feedback Loop	Time Line
Defining a quality high school program	Director of curriculum, standards, and articulation	Curriculum advisory committee with staff input	High school curriculum that provides quality four-year education for students and addresses state and national standards	CIC studies curriculum with input from staff CIC recommends changes and graduation requirements	Fall 2002 Dec. 2002

grade level, or team), and finally as a school community. Then participants can develop consensus regarding the target(s) they believe to be most realistic for the coming year. Participants should explain how these targets affect the following:

- Long-term growth consistent with district goals
- Professional development necessary to accomplish goals
- Tasks and meeting structures necessary to support those expectations

The questions help stakeholders make decisions about where to place the target for their site relative to overall district goals.

After developing school effectiveness plans and using a districtwide responsibility matrix for three years, one Thompson teacher sent this e-mail to a district administrator:

> Yesterday's math meeting with the elementary principals was one of the most exciting experiences of my 32-year career in the district. . . . I happened to pick up the Post-it notes [following our discussion]. All of the principals but one [changed their attitudes toward the proposed changes to the math program]. . . . I feel like we are making progress. I literally love the people I work with. . . . There is not the usual back-biting among the K–5, 6–8, and 9–12 levels. The leadership and listening we are getting from [administrators] is incredible.

It takes time to develop a commitment to a shared purpose. When push comes to shove, most of us fall back on what we know. If you want your classrooms to be places where learning happens, make certain that your students, parents, and staff are practicing, discussing, and reflecting about learning. Ask them what it looks like in action. Don't begin action planning by discussing what good schools or good *teaching* looks like. Begin by discussing what good *learning* looks like. Then make certain that people have equal access to the information they need to make sound decisions in terms of the learning target.

Making Data-Driven Decisions

Commitment to a shared purpose requires more than equal access to information; it requires equal access to the decision-making process itself. The Thompson School District has found that what Frankl (1959) said a half century ago still holds true today: the most fundamental choice human beings can make is choosing to be successful.

To make shared decision making work, your stakeholders must decide that all students can learn and that all stakeholders can play a significant role in the learning process. Then you need to give them information describing existing student performance so that they can make data-driven decisions that will drive appropriate change strategies. Your stakeholders need to know how and when decisions are made, as well as what their roles are in the process. This will make them more likely to support one another's efforts.

Thompson School District policy requires that all stakeholder groups be included in the decision-making process. It stipulates that the strongest voice in goal setting rests with parents and community members, the strongest voice in establishing curriculum standards and instructional strategies rests with staff, and the strongest voice in setting district priorities rests with the school board.

The site accountability advisory committee is responsible for goal setting within the parameters of the strategic plan. The SAAC monitors site progress toward goals according to various student subgroups: gifted and talented, minorities, special needs, high mobility, and other subgroups as required by state regulations and district policy. The district office uses this assessment information to plan professional development activities and coordinate support for site initiatives. While the SAAC provides advice about budgeting needs and similar matters, it does not make curriculum, instructional, or disciplinary decisions or participate in principal or staff evaluations.

The Thompson school board recognizes that written policies do not ensure equal access to information or to programs and services. That is why its shared decision-making manual includes a matrix of decision-making authority according to various topics. A summary of the major topics included in this matrix appears in Figure 3.5.

FIGURE 3.5	
Sample Decision-Making Matrix	
Decision Focus	**How and Where Decisions Are Made**
Curriculum	Site-based within articulated district standards
Assessment	Shared development of a consistent, districtwide process
Instructional delivery	Site-based decisions driven and refined through data analysis and coordinated by the district across grade levels
Accountability process	Shared development with ongoing analysis of results from the classroom to the boardroom
Budget and finance	Shared development of needs identified at the site level and driven by a comprehensive district process
Operational services	District coordination to meet site needs
Human resources	District coordination based on needs identified by sites
Communications	Varies by need and ramifications of subject matter

Regardless of personality differences, you raise the stakes for people when you ask them to put their plans into writing. Leaders should share in the responsibilities for creating the decision-making matrix so that stakeholders can see how their contributions affect district goals. You may also want to create a chart similar to the one in Figure 3.6, which shows how decisions are categorized and assigned. The particular appearance of the matrix and the flowchart is not significant; what's more important is that stakeholders discuss how they will work together to make decisions about the quality of learning and teaching in various venues. They will learn a great deal about one another through these discussions, and will probably avoid procedural disagreements that could jeopardize the connections between purpose and practice.

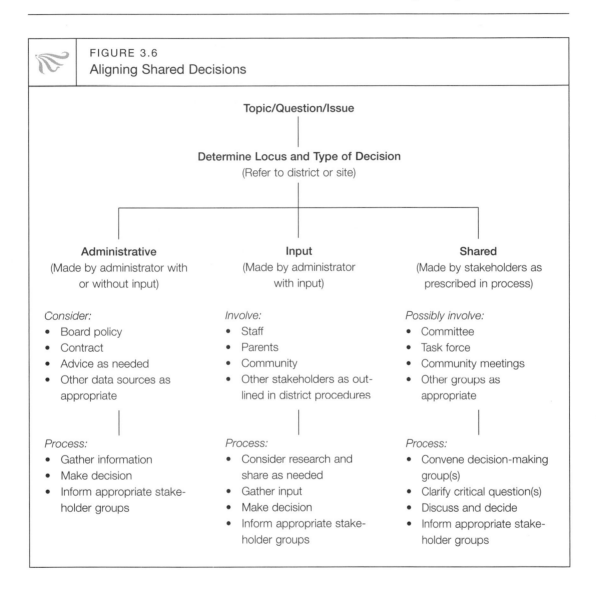

FIGURE 3.6
Aligning Shared Decisions

Topic/Question/Issue

Determine Locus and Type of Decision
(Refer to district or site)

Administrative	Input	Shared
(Made by administrator with or without input)	(Made by administrator with input)	(Made by stakeholders as prescribed in process)

Consider:
- Board policy
- Contract
- Advice as needed
- Other data sources as appropriate

Involve:
- Staff
- Parents
- Community
- Other stakeholders as outlined in district procedures

Possibly involve:
- Committee
- Task force
- Community meetings
- Other groups as appropriate

Process:
- Gather information
- Make decision
- Inform appropriate stakeholder groups

Process:
- Consider research and share as needed
- Gather input
- Make decision
- Inform appropriate stakeholder groups

Process:
- Convene decision-making group(s)
- Clarify critical question(s)
- Discuss and decide
- Inform appropriate stakeholder groups

Your stakeholders will not want to be involved in every decision, but you should not make assumptions about which decisions people will deem important. Teachers should generally be responsible for student achievement and well-being within their classrooms, principals should be responsible for *coordinating* student achievement and well-being within their schools, and district administrators should be responsible for *coordinating and articulating* student achievement and well-being from level to level.

Use the following rule of thumb to guide your decision-making process: *write it down.* Written goals and procedures develop trust and create a touchstone to guide daily practices until they can become organizational habits. Be certain that your process addresses the following questions:

- What parts of this decision rest with the district and what parts rest with the site?
- Is this an administrative, input, or shared decision?
- What stakeholder groups need to be involved in the decision-making process, and how and where should they be involved?
- Does the process provide for alternative procedures in emergency situations?

No system will eliminate all controversy. But the following description of the Thompson School District's experience with high school schedules provides an excellent example of how written guidelines can guide a school district until new decision-making skills can become a habit.

District administrators had been questioning the adequacy of student contact time in their five high schools for a couple of years. When the district was audited by the state, it stood to lose even more funding than administrators had expected. Unfortunately, just as the high school staffs were finally developing a more positive attitude toward an internal review of high school programs, the audit problem became public. The administrative team was concerned that a political debate involving high school parents and staff might derail this process.

The administrators knew that the district's decision-making matrix classified scheduling as an input decision to be made at each site, but the funding problem was not limited to a single site. They sought input from the five high school principals and made a decision that changed all high school schedules slightly, and one of them significantly. When this decision was challenged by students, parents, and staff at the school with the significantly altered schedule, district administrators cited all the appropriate guidelines from the decision-making manual, including the section that gave them the authority to act outside normal channels in "exceptional situations."

People were unhappy with the decision. However, most staff members agreed that the situation was serious enough to be considered "exceptional." One department chair photocopied the relevant section of the guide and distributed it to staff. He urged them to move beyond their disappointment and to accept that the process had been followed.

Decision-making matrices and flowcharts won't eliminate controversy, but they will provide a road map to help you navigate controversial situations in a fair and open manner according to commonly accepted criteria. They also offer a standard against which decisions can be evaluated, allowing you to align your stakeholders' daily practice with district goals. You can use matrices as guidelines for making information available to all stakeholders so that they can make data-driven decisions consistent with district goals and state and federal regulations. When your stakeholders help set decision-making standards, they will be more willing to accept decisions even when they do not like them.

Becoming Accountable for Results

Collaborative and focused reflection requires a common understanding of roles and responsibilities. It is derived from a shared purpose and is dependent upon equal access to information. To develop habits of collaboration and reflection, your stakeholders need to understand how to plan for, monitor, and adjust their strategies as they travel the challenging path from where they are to where they want to be. Bennis and Biederman (1997) suggest that while you can manage without being an effective leader, you cannot lead without being an effective manager. The key is to manage your district so that people can work together in positive ways.

The first two *Ps*—purpose and parameters—focus on management. Effective leaders establish management *parameters* that achieve the school district's shared *purpose*. There is stability in knowing where you are going and the general route you will take to get there. But not everybody begins the journey from the same point. You can use the third *P*—principles—to help people know how to plan appropriate routes from where they are, as well as effective detours in the event that the chosen road is inaccessible. This understanding is where leadership begins. Accountability is not about holding a hammer over stakeholders' heads; it is about establishing a link between their long-range goals and their daily practices.

In the early 1990s, school leaders in the Clear Creek School District in Idaho Springs, Colorado, used a "trainer of trainers" model to develop staff skills relative to learning styles and modalities, differentiated instruction, peer coaching, and the application of special education intervention techniques in the regular classroom. The training took one day each week for five weeks and included research, demonstrations, and guided practice. Following each session, participants were expected to implement new instructional strategies in their own classrooms. They were observed by their principals and were encouraged to practice peer coaching with another teacher in their building. In 1990, Clear Creek was one of eight districts nationwide to receive an award from the National Council of States on Inservice Education for research-based professional development.

The Clear Creek experience and the Glenview experiences mentioned earlier prove that teachers can implement change. Clear Creek was an example of shifting professional development from a passive "sit-and-get" process to a process developed and directed by teachers. The Glenview staff transformed professional development from a trainer of trainers model to a learning community model, where teachers and parents learned together. However, the disturbing fact of both models was the inability of the districts to sustain key changes over time. In both situations, district staff lacked the ability to gather and analyze data quickly enough to allow professional development decisions to be based on student achievement results. Professional development was focused on input—teaching—rather than output—learning.

In 2000, the Thompson School District raised professional decision making to a new level by shifting the focus of professional development from teaching to learning. Stakeholders no longer asked how successfully the district was implementing programs and services; instead, they asked to what extent those programs and services were having an impact on student achievement and well-being. The litmus test became learning, not teaching. For example, one elementary school principal, many of whose students came from homes in which English was a second language or from low socio-economic backgrounds, or both, used student achievement data to convince his staff that they could not teach students to think critically unless they learned to think critically themselves. That school developed a positive growth curve over a three-year period.

Successful schools hold themselves accountable for learning. However, if you want your staff to become accountable for student achievement and well-being, they need more than frequent and consistent feedback on student performance; they need the time and the skills to analyze the connections between their instructional decisions and student success, and the opportunities to reflect collaboratively about achievement targets, program and service successes, professional development opportunities, and resource allocations.

Most accountability processes are based on a deficit model: they ask stakeholders to identify their shortcomings and practice skills they do not currently have, and to identify teaching and administrative "stars" who learn new skills and then teach them to the masses. You can use the learning community model instead to help your stakeholders identify their own successes and to provide them with the time and resources they need to share successful practices across schools and eventually with other districts. But these analyses need to become more than celebrations of a program or strategy. They need to identify the underlying principles present in multiple examples of successful programs and services.

An accountability process does not give you or your stakeholders more time; it gives you a new focus so that you can use your time more effectively. Figure 3.7 illustrates the accountability process that the Thompson schools use to establish time lines and tasks and to ensure equal access to information.

FIGURE 3.7
Accreditation and Accountability Process

Time Line	Task/Document	People Responsible	Submission
August	*School Achievement Profile* Compilation of school's goals, demographics, attendance report, stability report, Colorado Discipline Report, Colorado Basic Literacy Act Report, achievement data, survey data, and graduation and dropout rates (high school only)	Office of assessment and student growth	Report supplied to school administrator
September	*School Action Plan* Review and analysis of data in the School Achievement Profile, consisting of a cover page and the following items for each school: • Completed Year-End Goals Summary (form supplied by assessment office)—summary of progress toward previous year's goals, accomplishments, and next steps • Completed RF-1 form, including budget recommendations to principal • Basic Skills Annual Target Plans—plans for reading, writing, and math • Critical Thinking and Creativity Annual Target Plan • Safety and Belonging Annual Target Plan • School-to-Life Annual Target Plan • AP classes and score reports (high school only)	School staff, administration, and site accountability advisory committee (SAAC)	Plan submitted to director of assessment and student growth Year-End Goals Summary distributed to SAAC and included in parent newsletter (Accreditation Plan, subsection C-7)
October	*Accreditation Monitoring and Review* School Action Plans reviewed by student achievemnet services (SAS) staff	Director of assessment and student growth, SAS directors	Report on monitoring/review of accreditation status of each school submitted to district accountability advisory committee (DAAC)

Timing	Report	Responsible	Action
October/November	*Accreditation Monitoring and Review* — Recommendations from district office reviewed by DAAC	DAAC	Recommendations for maintaining/revising accreditation status of schools made to boards of education (BOE)
November	*Accreditation Recommendation* — DAAC recommendations for accreditation reviewed by board of education	Superintendent of schools and DAAC	BOE will verify accreditation status of schools
December	*District Annual Accreditation Report to Community* — Report will include statutory requirements for schools and for district	Office of communications, office of assessment and student growth	Report distributed to community and to Colorado Department of Education
December/January	*Level Reports to Board of Education* — Report, which includes data required by accountability and accreditation statutes	Lead principals (data report prepared by office of assessment and student growth)	Dialogue with BOE in study session with accompanying written report prepared by Assessment Office
January	*Midyear Goals Summary* — Goals summary (form supplied by assessment office) of progress on current Annual Building Targets	School administrator	Summary submitted to director of assessment and student growth and distributed to SAAC
May	*Colorado Discipline Report* — Report by school, aggregated for district by level	Principals	Report given to director of assessment and student growth for submission to Colorado Department of Education
June	*Colorado Basic Literacy Act Report* — Report by school, aggregated for district by level	Principals	Report given to director of assessment and student growth for submission to Colorado Department of Education

Developing Leadership and Facilitation Skills

Merriam-Webster's dictionary (Merriam-Webster, 1991) defines the verb "to lead" as "to guide, especially by going in advance." You cannot tell stakeholders how to create quality. You must "go in advance." If you want to create quality schools, model quality leadership.

Leadership involves change, but it also requires stability. Your stakeholders need a place to stand, and a path from where they are to where they want to be. Otherwise, they cannot adjust the quality target to meet their next challenge.

In recent years, the term "management" has carried a negative connotation. It has implied a lack of creativity or a dependence on control and manipulation. But the mark of an effective leader is the ability to make happen the things that people want to happen. The long-range funding priorities plan is the last of the Four *P* protocols you need to make quality a habit throughout your school district. Funding priorities provide the ultimate connection between purpose and practice.

Your school district probably spends 80 to 85 percent of its budget on personnel. You can leverage your community's resources by focusing those dollars on clearly defined targets. How could you use the criteria listed in Figure 3.8 to paint your target?

Sharing information with stakeholders and gathering their responses are two important elements in gaining a broad commitment to a shared purpose. But unless your stakeholders see something happening as a result of their efforts, you cannot sustain their commitment over time. You and your school board can highlight how and where various stakeholder tasks have helped shape district goals and leverage resources toward achieving success for all students. The Thompson School District staff used the form in Figure 3.9 to gather information on successes across levels and departments.

The following testimonials from Thompson School District stakeholders provide some indication of why this approach works. They were offered to the superintendent at school board, advisory committee, and administrative meetings, and at luncheons with student government leaders. As you read them,

FIGURE 3.8
Elements of a Funding Priorities Plan

An effective funding priorities plan includes the following:

- A rationale stating why evidence was gathered on various programs and services, how the evidence was gathered, how it will be used, and how it will be communicated/stored/protected over time
- Evidence regarding the validity and reliability of data-gathering procedures
- Evidence that data-gathering procedures were designed, approved, and communicated before implementation of the program/strategy
- Evidence that in areas where people were asked to invent solutions rather than simply find known solutions, rubrics were designed to evaluate results before implementing the program/strategy
- Explanations of how opportunities were built into the evidence-gathering procedures to allow for consideration of unintended results
- Provisions for making data gathering and reporting as unobtrusive and user-friendly as possible
- Evidence that data-gathering techniques were coordinated consistently by and across levels (including computerized analysis, recording, and reporting of evidence where possible)

think about how they express the Four *P*s, and how they helped Thompson stakeholders determine how and when to move their quality target.

School Board Members

- Recommendations that come to us now include clear statements of priorities with accompanying rationale.
- More and more, our decisions are aligning yearly priorities with the district's strategic goals.
- We are getting better at including the community in our decision-making process.
- I now take for granted that budget recommendations will include supporting data about student achievement.
- Our administrators are doing a much better job of presenting unbiased information in a timely manner.

FIGURE 3.9
Long-Term Funding Priorities: Gathering Confirming Data

Gather Input by Level

School _____   Principal _____

Dates of advisory meetings _____   Number attending _____

Dates of staff meetings _____   Number attending _____

Who put this summary together? _____

1. Given the priorities identified at your level last year (see below), what still belongs on this list? Take into account where we are now and where we need to go in the future.

Please put in priority order (leave blank if an item should no longer be on the list):

_____   Increase noninstructional budget to offset costs of professional development and other items at the building level.
_____   Add counseling and administrative staff.
_____   Add academy staff.

2. What other issues should we consider to be funding priorities at this level to meet our needs in relationship to our strategic goals?

3. Identify other strongly held comments or opinions from the majority of the participants involved (indicate whether staff or advisory group):

Signatures:

Principal _____   Advisory Chair _____

Association Representative _____

Staff Members

- I am seeing veteran teachers more excited about learning than they have been in years.
- Teachers are constantly telling me about students who are getting excited about math since we have introduced these new thinking strategies.
- We've been talking about literacy skills, but these are really thinking skills.
- If money gets tighter, don't take away our literacy coaches or our book study groups. This is some of the best professional development we have ever had in this school district.
- Our team works because we have a common purpose, we hold expectations for ourselves and our students, we spend time analyzing our teaching strategies, and we hold one another accountable for the success of every student on this team.

Parents from Site Accountability Advisory Committees

- We don't need to spend a lot more time on how the SAAC should work. We need to spend it in feeder group meetings so we can share ideas.
- We have a lot of good things happening, but we need to spend more time sharing them.
- We need a job description for SAAC membership. We waste too much time getting people up to speed on their responsibilities. By the time we understand our responsibilities, we are moving with our kids to the next level.

Students

- I wish the high school teachers would share [state test] results with me the way the middle school teachers do.
- We need to let high school students know how important [state] test results really are. Then they would take the tests more seriously.

No amount of preplanning or warnings can prepare stakeholders for every quirk within a change process. Your job is to avoid an ambush or a sense of manipulation. Be sure to communicate the assumptions underlying your district's funding priorities effectively and repeatedly. While not every financial decision can be based on quantifiable data, school leaders can employ systematic procedures to gather evidence on the effectiveness of various programs and services.

You can use the four management protocols described in this chapter to provide a link between purpose and practice in your school district. Figure 3.10 provides a framework for doing so. As you proceed, be careful to ensure that your strategic planning, shared decision making, accountability, and funding priorities enhance rather than impede your community's progress toward sustaining quality schools. The protocols are means to an end, not ends in themselves. Use them to focus on people, beginning with students. Use them to ask questions, and listen to the answers. Ask yourself frequently, "Are people driving the process, or is the process driving people?"

FIGURE 3.10

Protocols for Making Quality a Habit

Fact-Finding Questions	Yes/No	Next Step
1. Do we have a written strategic plan?	Yes	Gauge the following: • Who was involved in development • Time parameter of plan • Extent to which it focuses on student achievement and well-being
	No	• Potential support among school district leaders (school board, administrators, teachers, and community) • Resources required to create a plan (see Chapter 2)
2. Do we have a written decision-making process?	Yes	Gauge the following: • Who makes major decisions • Roles and responsibilities of various stakeholder groups • Accessibility of programs and services
	No	• Potential commitment to shared decision making among district leaders (school board, administrators, teachers, and community) • Resources required to develop a plan (see Chapter 3)
3. Do we have a written account-ability process?	Yes	Gauge the following: • Accountability for major tasks within the strategic plan • Consistency with state and federal regulations • Extent to which decisions are data-driven
	No	• Potential commitment for a process among district leaders (school board, administrators, teachers, and community) • Resources required to develop an ongoing process (see Chapter 4)
4. Do we have a written plan for setting long-range funding priorities?	Yes	Gauge the following: • Relationship to strategic goals • Relationship to decision-making process • Relationship to actual budgeting practices • Extent to which process is self-monitoring
	No	• Potential support for a funding priorities plan among district leaders (school board, administrators, teachers, and community) • Resources required to develop a funding priorities plan (see Chapter 5)

4

Focusing on Success

Success begins with a change in expectations. It is sustained with a change in attitudes.

Susan works her way through a set of transparencies. She is the epitome of modern leadership, a leader on the cutting edge. It's the 1980s, and many superintendents are still focusing on Madeline Hunter's elements of instruction techniques (Hunter, 1969). But Susan is showing her staff district comparisons of their test scores by grade. Her focus is on output rather than input—student performance rather than teaching performance.

Susan points out discrepancies in student test scores from one classroom to another and asks staff members to think about the causes underlying various deficits. The murmuring in the audience, however, is not focused on student achievement but on several embarrassed teachers. This is a small school district with only one or two classrooms per grade in each school. Despite the fact that Susan has not named specific teachers, several red faces identify those whose students have not achieved district expectations.

Technology has made it possible for today's leaders to avoid the pitfalls that Susan experienced 20 years ago. With computers and advanced student data management software, teachers can review their own test scores and then investigate achievement trends with their colleagues. But one thing has not changed. In most school districts across the country, school leaders still focus school improvement efforts on addressing deficits in student performance—finding what is *not* working and *fixing* it.

Levine (2002) encourages parents and teachers to shift their thinking and work toward building on students' strengths. He cites examples of kids who believe that success means being like other kids instead of making the most of their unique way of thinking. He also discusses how adult expectations help create student social groups: popular students, controversial students, amiable students, neglected students, and rejected students. As one student leader suggested to me,

> You adults don't mean to do it. But you create more cliques than we do. The band director likes band kids. The coaches like the jocks. AP teachers like the geeks. And if I'm supposed to be the student government president representing all students, why do teachers tell me I shouldn't hang around with "those" kids?

It should be disturbing to educators that Levine's best-selling book about learning focuses on how parents and students must learn to "manage the system." While system-management skills are practical for both immediate and long-term learning, they are a bit of an indictment of us as school leaders. While we profess in our mission statements and our goals to be committed to meeting students' individual needs, we often create schools that define success as "learning to do things the right way." Because 65 to 70 percent of educators are Guardians, the "right way" involves following rules, listening, focusing on one issue at a time, and pleasing authority figures. This one-size-fits-all mentality tells students at a very early age who is smart and who is not.

Your school community will be successful when stakeholders expect *all* children to learn, and when they understand that children learn in different ways. What teachers and other adults tell kids is not nearly as important as what they model in their everyday practices. You will help your stakeholders model effective learning when you expect them to build on success rather than look for deficits—when you make school improvement a positive experience rather than a negative one.

An analysis of deficits draws people's attention to what is not working; it asks people to spend their entire career finding out how ineffective they have been. What kind of atmosphere does this create for teachers? What kind of attitude does it engender in classrooms? Remember, people "downshift" when they feel threatened or incapable of meeting expectations.

According to the Third International Mathematics and Science Study, student performance is more highly correlated with adult expectations than with an articulated curriculum or particular teaching strategies (Kroeze & Johnson, 1997). This does not mean that curriculum articulation and effective instructional strategies do not matter, but that you should help your stakeholders focus on success and model it. They will model learning more effectively if you can help them become a connected learning community. When you try to change your schools by fixing what is wrong, you create a focus on weakness rather than on success. Csikszentmihalyi (1990) suggests that people work most effectively when they know what they need to do, believe that they have the skills to do it, and receive feedback on how closely their efforts approximate their expectations.

Watching for Differences in Words and Actions

Stakeholders define quality schools in terms of their personal values. If you know what they value, you have a better chance of meeting their expectations. Let's think about how people's words and actions provide clues to what they value and to their sense of what constitutes success. The following paragraphs are adapted from *The Real Colors Homeowner's Guide* (Johnson, 2004). These are not absolute descriptions of individual personalities, but you can use them as gateways to understanding your stakeholders' expectations. As you read through these personality descriptions, focus on strengths rather than deficits. Think about how you could engage the different personalities in various aspects of a change process, and about where your own personality fits into this mix.

Idealists

Idealists are driven by their relationships with other people. Their words include references to purpose and connections. Idealists expect leaders to build personal connections that are peaceful and harmonious. Their tone, if not their words, tends to be questioning and inviting. But Idealists are not weak or incapable of taking a position. When Idealists' expectations are not met, they may at first ask, "Why can't administrators be more understanding?" If leaders don't respond to their subtle suggestions, they become more personal in their indignation: "I thought Ted's comment to Leslie was unforgivable." And when they become totally exasperated, they might say, "It's easier for me to stay in my classroom and pretend administrators simply don't exist." Idealists tend to be extremely personal both in their praise and in their wrath.

Guardians

Guardians are more interested in stability and rules. Their words generally include references to time management and parameters. They expect leaders to follow rules and provide rewards for a job well done. Guardians also expect leaders to make certain that others follow the rules. They will initially voice their concern by asking, "Why can't administrators be more responsible?" As they grow more agitated, they move to, "We need to talk with the district office about how principals fail to follow policy and procedures." And when they become totally exasperated, they might say, "Forget all that catching-flies-with-honey stuff—I'd like to catch my principal by the throat." Guardians focus on justice both in their praise and in their wrath.

Rationals

Rationals respect logic. They frequently refer to processes and "big ideas." As you listen for Rational clues, listen for words that connect to ideas and principles, and for a sense of awe about how things work. Rationals want to connect with others, but they think there would be little reason for strife in the world if people were less emotional. Their words tend to be questioning and exploratory. When leaders fail to meet Rationals' expectations, the leaders might hear, "Administrators just don't get it." In a more agitated state, they may become more pointed: "Because our principal isn't capable of reasoning through a problem situation, he resorts to childish tirades." And when they become totally exasperated, they might say, "My principal does not think; therefore, he is not." When Rationals' expectations go unmet, they may sound cold and arrogant.

Artisans

Artisans respect results, and place a priority on immediacy. Leaders do not need to listen closely for Artisan clues, because Artisans are direct and often unimpressed with roles and positions. Guardians often refer to Artisans as flighty or unfocused. Artisans seldom test the waters with their words; they are about action, believing that experience is the best teacher. Leaders fail to meet Artisans' expectations when they fail to act. At first, Artisans may use humor to make their point: "Administrators never saw a policy they didn't like." As they grow more agitated, their humor becomes more cutting and more action oriented: "The heck with catching flies with honey. My principal needs a flyswatter." And when they become totally exasperated, they might say, "The kindest thing my principal could do for Jim is to find him a new career."

When you see stakeholders doing "good" things, you want to encourage and reinforce them. But if you and your stakeholders define "good" things as those that feel comfortable to you, you may actually be short-changing your students, particularly Rationals and Artisans, who have few adult models to advocate for them in most school communities. In the long term, you may also be shortchanging Guardian and Idealist adults.

Figure 4.1 shows a letter from a successful teacher who lost the zeal to teach. How many such people have you lost in your school district?

FIGURE 4.1

A Letter of Resignation

Dear Mr. Travis,

I've been contemplating my resignation for some time now. I want you to know how much I have appreciated your support over these past three years. But I just don't get a thrill from my job anymore. Oh, I love the kids—if only I could spend more time with the kids. But I can no longer tolerate the bickering among the adults around here.

Most meetings with my team are more like open warfare. Don't get me wrong—they're good folks, and they try. We have made some progress lately: implemented some new differentiation strategies, gotten away from labeling kids, and even found some materials that the kids actually like. But it shouldn't always be this much of a struggle.

Every Sunday night I vow to have a positive week. And every Monday morning I find myself getting caught up in negative conversations. You know, "parents don't care, kids don't care, we don't have enough money or time"—that sort of thing. I guess we can change people's actions for a short time, but I'm not certain we can ever change their attitudes.

I feel guilty about abandoning you—and even more guilty about abandoning the kids. But I can't continue in a job that doesn't make me happy, and that actually brings me down. I don't want to become one of *them*. I know that sounds arrogant, but I don't know how else to say it. No wonder schools are such unhappy places. How can we expect the kids to be happy learners when we can't find joy as adults in what we do?

I wish you luck in changing the way schools work—for kids, I mean. If anyone can do it, you can.

Sincerely,

Bob

As you read Bob's letter, you may ask yourself, How can Mr. Travis "do it" if teachers like Bob keep leaving the profession? People like Bob are often valued initially for their ability to make connections with kids, but also criticized for their failure to become "team players"—more like us. If we don't encourage our staffs to value their own differences, how can we expect them to value differences in their students? You should help your stakeholders become more aware of the need for differences and more capable of engaging with rather than resisting them. Most people will work much harder to develop skills they find rewarding than they will to develop those they can never hope to master. Your stakeholders have been successful learners; your responsibility is to identify and support strategies that make them successful learning models for students.

Changing Attitudes

You probably don't stay awake at night conjuring up ways to make your employees miserable. In fact, you probably think you are doing the right thing when you show them how to do their jobs "better." After all, your employees should want to be successful—right? And if they don't learn more about whatever skill you consider to be lacking, they certainly won't be successful at it.

"Mistakes" are not always a factor in being at odds with your employees. Remember Laura and her Guardian colleagues from Chapter 3? Groupthink can be as detrimental to quality as open warfare. Quality requires a commitment to a shared purpose, but don't forget the need for data-driven decision making. The litmus test for success is the extent to which adults' actions promote learning—their own and their students'.

Responsibilities within a successful school or district are discharged through numerous short-term and daily tasks, including curriculum development, professional development, and student assessment. These ongoing tasks require ongoing coordination, probably by a standing committee of responsible stakeholders. But what happens to daily tasks such as lesson planning, unit planning, and team planning when no one is there to monitor individual and group behavior?

You cannot change people's personalities, but you can help them change their attitudes. Most people want to be around people who think and act the way they do, especially at work. We may be impressed initially with leaders who start out by bringing a spark to our situation, but their differences may eventually present challenges for us. If Bob challenges the status quo among parents and staff, he will soon learn how to fit into the group, become a loner, or (as in many cases) leave the profession. Such outcomes are true regardless of the profession; the status quo is the culture—the "way we do things."

A certain sense of "the way we do things" is important to any organization because it makes daily tasks more efficient. Too many possibilities can be difficult to manage. But when does too much rigidity become a detriment? Where is the balance?

You can help your stakeholders find a balance by seeing their differences as avenues to success rather than as roadblocks. Figure 4.2 illustrates a hierarchy of skills that you can use to help your stakeholders change their attitudes toward their individual and group differences. Column 1 lists Paul and Elder's (2002) intellectual standards for assessing thinking, Column 2 lists Chrislip's (2002) guide to collaborative practices, and Column 3 lists Hartzler and Henry's (1994) four areas of team fitness. You will need to provide professional development in these areas for your staff and community as they assume their responsibilities for making quality a habit in your school district.

Your stakeholders can use the following tactics to focus on success:

- **Strategic thinking** to translate individual successes with students and learning into a shared organizational *purpose*
- **Data-driven decision making** to focus on programs and services that have worked
- **Collaboration and reflection** to identify the learning/teaching *principles* underlying multiple success stories

FIGURE 4.2
Skills That Promote Connected Learning Communities

Thinking	Collaboration	Teaming
• Recognizing the purpose • Stating the question • Identifying assumptions • Identifying point of view • Gathering information and data • Identifying key concepts • Dealing with inferences • Considering implications and consequences	*Getting Started* • Analyzing the context • Deciding on a strategy *Setting Up for Success* • Identifying and convening stakeholders • Designing a process • Identifying information needs • Defining roles • Managing the process • Locating resources *Working Together* • Building • Engaging • Informing stakeholders • Deciding what needs to be done *Moving to Action* • Reaching out • Managing action	• Identifying and prioritizing customer focus • Clarifying direction in terms of customer expectations • Understanding individual and group strengths and weaknesses • Establishing accountability in terms of values, beliefs, and priorities

Source: These lists of skills were adapted from Chrislip (2002), Hartzler and Henry (1994), and Paul and Elder (2002).

• **Leadership and facilitation** to leverage resources toward expanding and refining successful practices across student subgroups

Though you will not be able to transform your entire school district into a team, you can encourage stakeholders to work as a collaborative, connected learning community. We will examine such teams in the next chapter, but for now let's focus on how you can help your stakeholders take success to a new level. Until your stakeholders recognize that they can either lament how others created their problems or work with what they've got, they will have difficulty letting go of the things that no longer serve their needs.

One day, Todd's principal asked him what he wanted to accomplish with his students that year. After listening to Todd's 30-minute oration, the principal asked Todd to list the three things he wanted to achieve, and immediately Todd realized how vague his plan actually was. When he began to berate himself for his lack of logic, however, his principal said, "You have to be kidding me. I wish I could see the big picture the way you do. I can see the logistical details, but I need you to paint the picture for me. Hey, we could make an effective team if we just had someone who could teach both of us to be a little more sensitive to people's feelings."

The principal took the time to see beyond Todd's lack of detail. He recognized that Todd brought one set of skills to the table and that he came to that table with a different yet equally valuable set of skills. He also recognized what else they needed to be successful.

The protocols described in Chapter 3 (strategic planning, shared decision making, accountability, and funding priorities) are designed to make quality a habit. But like any habit, organizational protocols don't simply happen. They are developed. Let's take a moment to consider what these organizational protocols look like in daily practice. What are staff and students doing when they are thinking strategically, when they are making data-driven decisions, and when they are reflecting collaboratively? What are you doing as a leader when you have facilitated an effective problem-solving process with your staff?

Take as an example the first habit, *strategic thinking*. The question that guides strategic thinking is "What should students know and be able to do as a result of their school experience?" Ask yourself what your schools would look like if staff and students were thinking strategically:

- What would students and teachers be doing in the classroom?
- What would team leaders and department chairs be doing to coordinate this kind of thinking?

- What kinds of conversations would be occurring at staff meetings?
- What would principals be doing to promote such conversations across schools?
- What would district office administrators be doing to facilitate these conversations across the school district?

Figure 4.3 provides a framework for encouraging strategic thinking across your school district's organizational structures.

Strategic thinking requires your stakeholders to identify students' needs, translate these needs into district goals, and focus on modifying programs and services to meet the needs. Strategic thinking creates the *probability* of addressing district goals in multiple ways. This in turn creates a need for

FIGURE 4.3
Questions That Promote Strategic Thinking

Structure	Questions to Ask
Classroom	Given what stakeholders know about learning, how would they frame their expectations within each classroom?
Department/Grade	Given stakeholders' expectations for various classrooms, how would they reframe their beliefs about what students need to know and be able to do as a result of their experience within a department/grade?
Building	Given stakeholders' expectations for various departments/grades, how would they reframe their beliefs about what students need to know and be able to do as a result of their experiences within a building?
Level	Given stakeholders' expectations for various buildings, how would they reframe their beliefs about what students need to know and be able to do as a result of their experiences in elementary, middle, or high school?
District	Given stakeholders' expectations for various levels, how would they reframe their beliefs about what students need to know and be able to do as a result of their preK–12th grade experiences?

each site to have a shared focus so that it can create realistic targets for student achievement and well-being. To emphasize your community's commitment to a shared purpose, you need to translate districtwide goals into manageable targets. Realistic targets require chunking of information that will make your stakeholders' work more manageable. People form habits when their actions bring about expected results over time. Your stakeholders won't mind working toward an achievable target, especially if they can use their strengths as a jumping-off point.

But what happens when the programs and services you implement do not achieve your intended purpose? In the parameters/political model of change, stakeholders search for mistakes and try to eliminate them; in the Four Ps model, we search for successes and try to replicate them in other venues.

You can use the Four Ps to help your stakeholders transform strategic thinking into a shared purpose. When your stakeholders hold themselves personally accountable for results, they will want to make certain that district resources are allocated to programs and services that work. Figure 4.4 illustrates how strategic thinking leads to a shared focus that encourages all stakeholders to become personally accountable for leveraging resources appropriately. Student needs drive district goals; district goals establish individual and group targets for yearly performance benchmarks; yearly benchmarks drive analyses of individual and group actions relative to student achievement results; and those analyses identify the successful practices that drive the allocation of district resources. When your stakeholders think strategically in terms of a shared focus, they will see that they can become personally accountable for leveraging programs and services toward achieving success for all students.

Developing a Shared Purpose

Your stakeholders should work as a collaborative learning community for three reasons: to create a balance between the internal and external personalities in your school community, to establish a common purpose for learning, and to model effective learning across organizational structures.

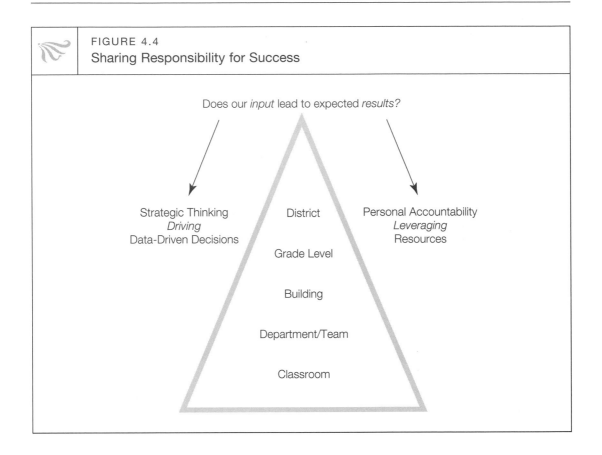

FIGURE 4.4
Sharing Responsibility for Success

Does our *input* lead to expected *results?*

Strategic Thinking
Driving
Data-Driven Decisions

District

Grade Level

Building

Department/Team

Classroom

Personal Accountability
Leveraging
Resources

A strategic plan involves more than creating general statements that address the mission, goals, and vision of a school district. Ninety to 95 percent of most school staffs approach learning from either a purpose or a parameters perspective. Of these, 25 to 30 percent are Idealists who ask, "Why is this program or service important?" and 65 to 70 percent are Guardians who ask, "What are the rules for making decisions about programs or services?" At the same time, 40 to 45 percent of the adult stakeholders outside the schoolhouse walls are more focused on matters of principles and priorities: 35 to 40 percent are Artisans who ask, "Will the programs or services work?" and fewer than 5 percent are Rationals who ask, "How will the school district monitor and adjust daily practices?"

Idealists require different assurances than Guardians, who require different assurances than Rationals, who require different assurances than Artisans. Our public schools are filled with good people who are doing what they do effectively. But all too frequently they lack the management protocols that encourage strategic thinking—a Rational task. In order to link purpose to practice, you need to ask your stakeholders, "Are the things that we do well preparing students for success in the real world?" Purpose without a plan does not ensure quality schools. However, a plan without a purpose is little more than busywork.

You can help your stakeholders become a collaborative learning community by asking critical questions to clarify community values about schools and learning, summarizing and verifying what you've heard, and painting a clear target.

Phase 1: Clarifying Community Values About Schools and Learning

The first phase in developing a collaborative learning community is about defining quality—establishing community values and expectations. It seeks answers to two questions: What is the purpose of schooling, and what should children know and be able to do as a result of schooling?

You can conduct dialogues with your community through a series of geographically dispersed meetings to identify community values. Community dialogues are more effective than paper-and-pencil surveys alone because they provide opportunities for leaders to hear the emotions and the convictions behind stakeholders' preferences. They also give stakeholders an opportunity to hear one another firsthand rather than read a summary of responses. Surveys can be used to generate thinking before the dialogue sessions, but the advantages of face-to-face communication should not be underestimated. The key to a successful community dialogue lies in both the organization of the session and the ability of the leaders to listen to stakeholders rather than present information to them. You can use Figure 4.5 to guide your community dialogues.

Effective community dialogue requires effective facilitation. You can train principals and directors to facilitate dialogue by modeling the process as

FIGURE 4.5
Community Dialogue Guidelines

Preparing for the dialogue:

- Train principals/operational directors to facilitate staff and community advisory group discussions at their sites.
- Gain school board members' commitments to observe sessions without limiting or controlling group discussions.
- Prepare meeting agendas.
- Advertise the purpose, place, and time of dialogue sessions.
- Prepare session materials (questions, flipcharts, markers, stickers, and snacks).
- Train dialogue facilitators and reporters.

Conducting the dialogue:

- Superintendent welcomes participants and sets tone of openness and optimism, pledging to honor input.
- Coordinator provides directions for the evening: small-group work, reporting, prioritizing ideas.
- Small mixed groups of parents, staff, and other community members respond to discussion questions.
- Groups report.
- Superintendent thanks people for coming, pledges to provide meeting summary to all schools to be shared with stakeholders, and explains timetable for remaining steps before seeking school board approval of a strategic plan.
- Coordinator distributes 10 stickers to each participant and asks them to place their stickers on the item(s) that they believe to be most important. (Participants may place all stickers on one item or spread them over several items.)

you gather their input. Distribute the questions to principals and directors before an administrative meeting. At the meeting, place the participants in like groups—elementary principals, middle school principals, high school principals, support service directors, and so on. If you have a large district, use district office staff to assist you. To be most effective, be certain that these administrators know that their input will become a part of the district's overall input for developing strategic goals.

You should structure community dialogues to avoid the slightest hint of control or manipulation. Make information readily available to all participants so that the meeting atmosphere encourages honesty and risk taking. In the Glenview School District in Illinois, leaders sent the following questions to teachers, administrators, and community advisory groups at each school site before conducting the community dialogue sessions:

- Can you put our mission statement into your own words?
- What should our students know and be able to do in order to achieve this mission?
- To what extent is what students do every day in school helping them achieve our mission?
- How are you responsible for student achievement and well-being?

Effective community dialogue sessions take the table to the people rather than simply inviting people to the table. It is not enough to open the schoolhouse doors to all comers or even to invite all stakeholders to attend school meetings. Artisans do not typically feel welcome in school environments, where their inclination toward action and risk taking is often perceived as impetuous. You need to take the dialogue sessions to the community. If your district has more than one high school feeder area, you may also want to avoid meetings by feeder groups. This approach avoids positioning by cutting across groups that might see themselves as competitors. You may also want to hold special meetings or luncheons—again, taking the table to the people.

Jack, a school superintendent, went out of his way to gain credibility with two groups that are frequently left out of the strategic planning loop: former school board members and administrators, and people who have had negative experiences with the schools. Jack scheduled two luncheon meetings with the former school board members and administrators to assure them that the planning process would evolve from past successes (assets) rather than mistakes (deficits). He asked for their historical perspective and pledged to share results with them following the dialogue sessions.

Jack also met with several parents individually. He knew those stakeholders were generally supportive of the schools but had had one or more negative experiences with staff. Those individuals appreciated Jack's "bringing the table to them," and they shared their experiences with other parents. One individual later ran successfully for the school board, citing Jack's willingness to reach out to disaffected citizens as a key reason for his decision to run.

There is a fine line between being positive and being a Pollyanna. You can focus on success without ignoring problems. Hear the issues, identify the successes, and develop promising practices as potential solutions to problems in other areas. Effective leaders like Jack have the confidence to find solutions anywhere and accept advice from multiple sources.

Phase 2: Summarizing and Verifying What You've Heard

Don't assume that you have captured the will and intent of the community without some form of verification. Before developing long-term strategies, ask, "Did we summarize your input correctly?" Again, your responsibility is not only to ask the right questions, that also to listen to people's answers. You should ask each school staff and community advisory committee to respond to this question in writing to allow the building principals, accountability advisory committee chairs, and teacher association representatives from each site to verify that they agree with or have corrected your interpretations of their input. The verification phase allows you to do several things:

- Ascertain that the goals and underlying principles of the strategic plan are consistent with stakeholders' expectations for schools and learning
- Make certain that stakeholders understand the potential impact of their expectations—that is, what it is that they are responsible for
- Signal the school district's commitment to an open planning process
- Establish consistency between purpose in words and purpose in action
- Signal a shift from an individual to a shared purpose

Don't protect stakeholders from the truth. Numerous organizational structures and procedures have a significant impact on their ability to achieve the district mission. For example, to implement the strategic plan, you may need to adjust both curriculum and instructional strategies. Curriculum issues involve *alignment:* curriculum focus years, high school course offerings, graduation requirements, and so on. These issues, in turn, lead to instructional delivery questions about developmentally appropriate practices, student scheduling, and transitions from level to level. Obviously, both curriculum and instructional delivery issues require funding for professional development, assessment, and two-way communication to ensure that all stakeholders have access to the process. Your stakeholders need to understand that behind every district goal lies a myriad of tasks.

Phase 3: Painting a Clear Target

The third phase of strategic planning is about responding to community expectations. If you are going to help your stakeholders find success, you need to find ways to focus on a few tasks that have the greatest potential for success. You can paint a clear target by asking the following questions:

- What would schools look like if all children were successful?
- How can each stakeholder group contribute toward this vision?
- What are the tactical matters related to these responsibilities?
- How can we realistically organize these tasks?
- What reports, processes, or programs will result from each task?

This is where you set the standards for success. You paint the target by outlining responsibilities, tasks, time lines, and expectations for those who sign on to the vision. You can use the matrix in Figure 4.6 to decide where to begin. For each task, ask your team to indicate whether it requires low effort or high effort from the staff and community. Then ask if successful completion of the task will have a low or high impact on student achievement and well-being.

FIGURE 4.6
Matrix for Improving the Odds for Success

	Low Impact	High Impact
Low Effort		
High Effort		

Some people will want to start with low-effort projects even if the impact of these projects is also low. Low-effort/high-impact projects are often hard to find. The starting point itself is not as important as stakeholders' understanding of what they are agreeing to do—they will be more patient and persistent if they know what to expect. It is one thing to know what success looks like; it is another thing to know what it entails in terms of time and energy. Communication involves more than just publishing a plan.

In the Thompson School District, the school board decided to make its strategic plan available to all stakeholders in print and on the district Web site. The board referenced it on a regular basis at school board, staff, and advisory committee functions. To keep the strategic plan dynamic, each school site developed a yearly action plan that included biennial reporting of results (midyear and end of year). The action-planning process provided connections between the community's intended purpose and its purpose-in-action, as well as between and among sites and between sites and the district as a whole.

Sharing Information

Conflict is a natural part of effective decision making. Goodlad, Mantle-Bromley, and Goodlad (2004) suggest that education in a democracy requires leaders to consider the political context in which decisions are made. Managed effectively, conflict gives rise to critical thinking and creativity. However, for group differences to have a positive effect on student achievement and well-being, you must promote and support total access to information about your programs and services. You must also recognize that differences in roles, responsibilities, skills, and attitudes strengthen teams. On the basis of their work with the National Network for Educational Renewal, Clark and Hughes (1995) report five characteristics necessary for successful partnerships. These characteristics, summarized in Figure 4.7, provide a set of guiding principles for shared decision making in any setting.

Most of these points have already been discussed. But why do they matter? What effect does an open planning and decision-making model have on students? In the following story, Anna, an extremely bright, very independent

---

FIGURE 4.7
Five Characteristics of Successful Partnerships

Shared decision making leads to effective decisions when

- All stakeholders have equal access to knowledge and information;
- Daily practices recognize and honor diversity;
- Decision-making practices model democratic ideals;
- The process reaches beyond school personnel to include students, parents, and other community members; and
- All stakeholders recognize the school's role as a partner in promoting and sustaining a quality community.

Source: Adapted from Clark and Hughes (1995).

learner who found her high school too confining, explains what happens when schools focus too much on control of information and create an attitude that certain groups have more expertise than others:

> At my old high school, I never understood the purpose of most classroom assignments. And it really used to bug me that all the other kids just seemed to do the work because that's what their parents and the teachers told them to do. They never asked why. Now that I can take more classes at the community college, I'm excited about learning. I never knew school could be this fun. My teachers get to know me. They respect my opinions—and even ask for them. They're also not afraid to say they don't know all the answers. I wish more kids would have the opportunity to take community college classes. But I guess most of them really don't want to take the chance. They have their plans all made—or they think they do. I wonder what will happen when they discover what they really want to do with their lives. I wonder if they ever really will. Or will they simply keep waiting for someone else to tell them what to think and when to think it?

In a political culture, problem solving focuses more on what will sell to various power groups than on what will have the most desirable effect on students and learning. It becomes what Roberts (2000) describes as maintaining control, winning, and avoiding embarrassment. When stakeholders represent their particular constituents, problem solving becomes political jockeying—it becomes a search for a political resolution to stakeholder conflicts rather than for solutions to issues of student achievement and well-being.

The community dialogue should be about critical thinking rather than selling ideas. It should focus on Heifetz's (1994) questions regarding stress: looking for the history behind apparent disagreements, examining how the organization may be promoting tension, considering how much stress a community can handle at any given time, and determining whether or not the disagreements may actually be designed as a means of avoiding the real issues. As one school board member said after listening to Anna's story, "I wish our parents and teachers could have heard Anna. We spend so much time talking at or around one another without asking the really critical questions. When we do ask questions, I'm not certain that we really listen to other people's answers. We're too busy listening for the answers we want to hear."

Differences sometimes lead to conflict. But that conflict can actually be a useful aspect of problem solving if you try to manage it rather than resolve it. Conflict resolution places the group's focus on solving political differences rather than viewing the problem from different perspectives. Susan, an effective group facilitator, responded to one dialogue participant in this way: "That is a great perspective of the issue at hand. How can we create a solution that addresses your concern without negating what Bill just said?"

You can help your stakeholders take responsibility for communicating prior to, during, and after decisions have been made. This approach builds an expectation that information will be shared within and between buildings and departments, and across all organizational structures. School leaders should establish procedures and time lines for routine communication and make certain that stakeholders know and understand them; they should also institute a two-way system of communication between the internal and external publics. External communication should include midyear and year-end reports completed according to district guidelines. In addition, parents and community members should be informed of conference and report card dates, and made aware of communications and complaint procedures.

Developing a shared purpose requires equal access to information and equal opportunity to ask questions. It also requires assurances that all stakeholder groups have a place at the decision-making table. In any situation, some individuals have a deeper understanding of the information than others, but even the deepest understanding does not necessarily entitle individuals or groups to make the final decision. For example, most parents do not believe that they have more understanding of curricular issues than teachers or administrators. At the same time, most school personnel realize that their knowledge base relative to curriculum and instruction will have a much greater effect on student achievement if it is combined with parents' understanding of and commitment to a shared purpose. The question is not whether people should listen to one another but how and when players should yield to others. Different voices may carry more weight in one situation than in another.

To ensure that all voices can be heard, you can help schools create action plans through a process similar to that used by the district to create the strategic plan. Each action plan should address the following questions:

- What should our school do for children?
- What should children know and be able to do when they leave our school?
- To what extent is what students do every day in school helping them achieve our mission?
- What would our school(s) look like if all children were successful?
- How am I responsible for student achievement and well-being?
- What reports, processes, or programs should result from our work?

A shared focus requires a commitment to making information equally accessible to all stakeholder groups. Your strategic plan creates a blueprint for excellence, but it is only useful to individuals who can access it. Access depends on all stakeholders understanding the rules of the game. Heifetz (1994) suggests that leaders should not assume that problems, once solved, stay solved forever. When you create a shared decision-making environment, you increase the probability that your stakeholders will monitor programs and services so that success can be sustained over time and across student subgroups.

Becoming Accountable for Collaboration and Reflection

Your accountability plan may be strictly a local endeavor, or it may be part of a larger state requirement for school district accreditation. Many states now stipulate several conditions that school districts must satisfy in order to become accredited. In Colorado, for example, these conditions require that school districts provide assurance of the following:

- District content standards
- Indication of how standards, goals, and requirements are to be met through an accreditation plan
- Description of assessments used to measure student progress
- Goals and strategies designed to improve achievement for all students
- Indication of rigorous assessment procedures
- Commitment to meeting or exceeding state model content standards
- Establishment of a school review process
- Recognition of success and procedures for intervening in unsuccessful schools
- Corrective action procedures
- Communication with and involvement of stakeholders

To encourage personal accountability for a shared focus, your school board should adopt content standards for specific courses of study. These content standards should be statements describing what students should know and be able to do relative to a particular strategic goal. The board then needs to communicate a commitment to making data-driven decisions about which programs and services are most effective in helping students achieve those district standards. Key elements of the Thompson accountability process are listed in Figure 4.8.

Once your stakeholders understand their roles in and responsibility for sustaining quality throughout the entire school system, they need to understand how their work relates to the work of other groups. Who is accountable for goal setting, curriculum development, differentiating instructional delivery, and developing multiple assessments of student achievement and well-being? Better said, who is accountable for which aspects of each function, to whom are they accountable, and what are the results that will indicate

FIGURE 4.8

Key Elements of the Thompson School District's Accountability Program

Personal accountability ensures continuous growth by

- Revising districtwide curriculum in a systematic manner to ensure a standards-based program;
- Ensuring access for *all* students by differentiating instruction to meet the needs of students with varying backgrounds and abilities; and
- Developing multiple assessments that measure individual student and identified subgroup progress toward achieving district goals.

acceptable performance? You can set the stage for such analyses through your responsibility matrix and site action plans.

Under the best of circumstances, an accountability process is complex and difficult to manage. To further complicate the situation, approximately 75 percent of your taxpayers will have little direct interest in many school issues because they do not have school-age children.

Your school committees and task forces are probably stacked (unintentionally) with Guardians who are very effective at task analysis and Idealists who are very effective at establishing positive relationships. Unfortunately, this makeup often leaves such groups short of analytical skills and hesitant to consider options that lie outside traditional approaches to learning and teaching. You will need to help these groups understand their responsibilities relative to critical thinking, creativity, and accountability.

Establishing a dynamic accountability process that moves your stakeholders beyond compliance issues to issues of quality is vital. Though your entire school community cannot function as a team, it can become a collaborative learning community. Figure 4.9 illustrates how an effective accountability cycle works to create a shared purpose for learning.

If your accountability process is truly data driven, you will be able to identify programs and services that promote quality schools. An effective accountability process helps stakeholders focus on finding success and replicating it.

FIGURE 4.9
Sample Accountability Cycle

START

Site Action Planning

1. Staff reviews previous year's goals and student data.
2. Staff identifies successes and possible correlates with program/service changes and/or professional development.
3. Staff researches and develops new delivery strategies.
4. Staff develops action plan goals with subgroup expectations (plan format similar to responsibility matrix with district support requested and allocation of budget and professional development time).

Planning for Ensuing Year

1. Various committees report information to district office or other groups as charged.
2. District office uses evidence gathered from midyear report, committee reports, etc., to create responsibility matrix and shares with advisory committee.

District Review of Site Plans

1. District office staff conducts compliance review of plans, followed by quality review.
2. Staff identifies patterns of performance and needs by level.
3. Staff reports findings to advisory committee, and committee prepares accreditation recommendation to school board.

Midyear Update

1. District office staff reviews assessment data with principals by level.
2. District office staff and principals prepare progress report for school board review.
3. School board meets with principals by level to ask questions and show support.
4. Board asks for updates and/or adjustments to action plans.

Leading by Leveraging Resources

How is it that two people with very similar personalities can see the world from such different perspectives? Perhaps the story told by Mrs. Wallenda following the death of her husband, the famous acrobat, offers some insight here. When asked what her husband did differently on the day he fell to his death from a wire, Mrs. Wallenda responded, "Instead of focusing on walking the wire, he was thinking about not falling." The things that we choose to focus on have a tremendous effect on what we see.

To build an attitude of success, you must help your community shift its funding priorities process from building philosophical and political coalitions to identifying programs and services that work. Though you may not be able to gather quantifiable data for every decision, you can take the following steps as a means of leveraging resources toward district priorities:

- Agree on your criteria for success before implementing any program or service review.
- Insist on valid and reliable data-gathering techniques (valid and reliable data have significance to the process at hand and are collected in a prescribed, systematic manner).
- Report and analyze all data, including unintended learning or effects.
- Ensure that data are collected, communicated, and stored in ways that enhance analyses and protect people's privacy.

Budget preparations do not begin with numbers. They begin with goals and should conclude with a review of results. If your community is like most school communities, your stakeholders probably view the budgeting process as a way of identifying new needs. That is, they assume that all new programs and services will be considered in addition to rather than in place of existing programs and services. They expect "new" money to pay for new projects. This is not an effective process for leveraging resources.

Because public school funding streams are inconsistent at best, you may have difficulty establishing long-term projections of revenues and expenditures.

But you can use effective learning models in your school district to set funding priorities, which help people make concrete connections between their daily practices and the school district's long-term purpose. You can use these connections to build a budget that supports programs and services that work in your community and make success accessible to all students.

In Chapter 3 we reviewed the data-gathering memo that Thompson leaders send to their schools each year. You can use a similar format to help your staff analyze how effectively programs and services are working in your district. Then you can use this information to start a conversation with your school board based on evidence amassed by the people on the front lines—your staff and site accountability advisory committees. Thompson summarizes information from its schools as outlined below. A summary of priorities is a concrete example that you are not only listening to your stakeholders but are also acting on their input. Even if their particular concern has not made the final list, the list itself legitimizes the process. Those stakeholders who have participated in various dialogues about school district programs and services will probably see at least one item that came forward from their group.

What might be included in your school district's list of priorities? Think about how you might prepare a summary for your school board similar to the one in Figure 4.10 so that the public can see how the board sets the district's funding priorities.

Finding Success and Replicating It

With the availability of sophisticated data analysis software and communication technologies, it is becoming increasingly feasible to share practical information with all stakeholder groups. When you share information, you make it possible for everyone to become responsible for success. You might want to consider some of the following communication strategies:

- A yearly planning calendar indicating major tasks from the strategic plan to be discussed at advisory group and school board meetings

FIGURE 4.10
Thompson School District's Funding Priorities Summary

- Districtwide
  - Curriculum Improvement Council reorganization
  - Educational options (summer school and credit recovery programs)
  - English as a second language (staffing)
  - Counseling volunteer program (staffing)
  - Gifted and talented education

- Elementary school
  - Technology assistance
  - Literacy and mathematics coaches

- Middle school
  - Literacy coaches
  - Alternative education

- High school
  - Administrative assistance (staffing)
  - Alternative education (staffing)

- High school (*continued*)
  - Special education (administrative staffing)
  - Video services (internship positions)
  - Media services (staffing)

- Districtwide requests common to all levels
  - Noninstructional budget increase

- Operational services
  - Technologists
  - Heating and ventilation technician
  - Upgrading of high school building technology positions
  - Bus driver

- Business services (no requests)

- Human resources
  - At-risk program coordinator

- A single notebook that includes your strategic plan, shared decision-making manual, accountability plan, list of funding priorities, major district committee charges from the school board, and major communications tools and time lines
- A monthly memo from the superintendent that frames monthly issues in terms of critical questions and indicates whether they will be discussion or action items
- A monthly evaluation update with the superintendent and school board to model reflection-in-action
- Community luncheon meetings with key communicators, district displays at major community events, and a quarterly district electronic newsletter

Before we turn to the fifth step that brings us closer to quality schools, take a moment to reflect on your own school environment by answering the questions below.

1. How effectively do you use student assessment information within your action planning process?
2. Does your school board establish clear accountability parameters through yearly charges to major district committees, and do those committees know their relationships to one another as well as to the board?
3. Does your district have a process for developing action plans consistent with the strategic plan?
4. Which of the following words describes the history of change in your district? (List examples.)

   - Rapid
   - Slow to nonexistent
   - Effective
   - Ineffective

5. How do your major district committees function—independently, collaboratively, or as a single team?
6. To what extent have you become a connected learning community? What is your evidence? Where do you go from here?
7. What steps might you take to develop a responsibility matrix in your district along with a school effectiveness plan review rubric?
8. What might the accountability process look like in your district, and how do you begin your conversations?

Managing Tasks and Leading People

Managers do things right. Leaders do the right things.

—Warren Bennis

Is your school district traditional or cutting-edge? Are you child centered or committed to academic rigor? If you find these questions to be unfair, argumentative, or simplistic, you are well on your way to thinking in terms of the Four *P*s. Quality schools are not either/or organizations. If they become "a little bit of this and a little bit of that," they are not organizations at all. Quality schools require both direction and flexibility. They are both caring and rigorous. They are not amenable to quick fixes.

In this chapter, we consider how you can manage various tasks throughout your school district in order to lead evolutionary change. A business can tailor its goods and services to meet the needs and expectations of a portion of the general public—a portion large enough to make the business profitable. Businesses that can no longer meet the needs of their customers either change or wither. Public schools, however, have not been designed to satisfy a niche market. The public expects school officials to meet the needs of *all* students— a fundamental premise of education within our democracy. The change process in the public school arena does not differ significantly from nonpublic sector situations except that it evolves in the open. Success in a public arena requires dynamic, balanced leadership that manages tasks and leads people. It is easier to change the way you organize a task than it is to change people. It is important to have a plan, but it is also important to know when to adjust it to meet others' expectations.

Most people agree that improving student achievement and well-being is more likely to occur in a positive, consistent environment than in a stressful one. Yet some of the most widely suggested solutions for improving our public schools seem to be based on changing people. Such change ensures little more than a new set of power struggles. Rather than attaining what Quinn (1996) calls "deep change" that can be sustained over time, we too often take a flavor-of-the-month approach to reform. Instructionally, we have tried new math, whole language, problem-based learning, and so on. Organizationally, we have explored management by objectives, strategic planning, shared decision making, visioning, and more. And politically, we have drawn battle lines regarding merit pay, charter schools, and vouchers. With each such change we ask people to change their fundamental beliefs and practices. While each of these approaches has brought positive results in some schools and school districts, the overall mismatch between intent and actions continues to plague our public schools.

The focus of most change efforts, wherever they occur, depends on several factors, including the people who are leading the process, their conscious and unconscious beliefs, the breadth of their experience, and the depth of their knowledge about the issues at hand. At the same time, leaders function within a culture. Generally, it takes a different set of skills (or at least a different mix of them) to be successful in one culture than it takes in another. You may establish excellent relationships with people inside the schoolhouse walls and have poor communication with your external community, or vice versa.

For most people, change of any kind can be frightening, especially if they feel little or no sense of control over the change process. However, you are more likely to build a commitment to a shared purpose among stakeholders if you commit to the following principles:

- That all individuals have inherent value as contributing members of the organization
- That the fundamental purpose of change is to create an organizational structure that makes the most of everyone's talents
- That organizational success depends on individual success

Balanced leadership is about creating "deep change" that can be sustained over time, and about building connections that celebrate differences as a key to building quality schools. You can move beyond the flavor-of-the-month approach to reform by managing tasks so that your stakeholders achieve what Hartzler and Henry (1994) refer to as the four functions of effective teams:

- Identifying and prioritizing a customer focus
- Clarifying a direction in terms of customer expectations
- Understanding individual and group strengths and weaknesses
- Establishing accountability for established values, beliefs, and priorities

As you look at Figure 5.1, ask yourself where you are on your journey toward quality schools. Have you introduced your stakeholders to the Four Ps? Do they understand them? Have they learned to ask the Four P questions? Have they made quality a habit? Do they focus on success? If so, you are ready to consider how to manage tasks and lead people. As you think about this journey, consider how you might have managed tasks to lead a team of folks like the retirees described in the next several paragraphs.

Four very special, very different teachers are retiring tonight. It seems as though the entire community has come out for their send-off. "They have become an institution in this town," says

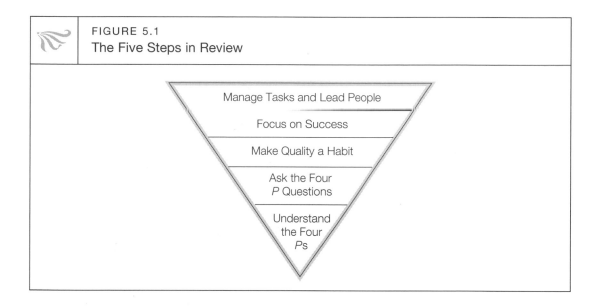

FIGURE 5.1
The Five Steps in Review

Manage Tasks and Lead People

Focus on Success

Make Quality a Habit

Ask the Four
P Questions

Understand
the Four
*P*s

Bob Elder, who graduated from high school 21 years ago and now has a son on the varsity track team. "You might love them, fear them, or just stay out of their way. But you certainly have to respect every one of them."

Janice is retiring after 30 years in the classroom. She taught 9th grade social studies, and most of her students adored her. Janice's principal, Mrs. Connor, liked her too, but she often had to pick up the pieces when Janice was sarcastic with a sensitive student or parent. Janice liked to push kids to think for themselves. She frequently told off-color stories in class to get students' attention. "What was on your mind when you were 14 years old?" she would frequently ask Mrs. Connor. Janice was and still is a rebel—whether in the classroom or at staff meetings. Someone will certainly include a story from one of her staff party escapades during tonight's retiree roast. It will be an acceptable story for mixed company if they leave out some of the details. Besides, most people in the community already know about the police holding Janice at the station that night. That story has almost become a community legend.

Mr. Anderson—his first name is Dave, but even Mrs. Connor called him Mr. Anderson—taught biology and chemistry. Few students were ever afraid of Mr. Anderson. They were more in awe. School legend has it that Mr. Anderson dropped out of medical school during his last year because his father died. He was always a loner. No one knew how Mrs. Anderson put up with his strange ways. No one talked in Mr. Anderson's room unless he called on them, and they always wanted to give the right answer—not because they were afraid of him, but because getting Mr. Anderson's approval was almost like winning a scholarship to Harvard. As a matter of fact, many students who took biology and chemistry with Mr. Anderson won scholarships to prestigious universities. Everyone wonders if Doc Helton will be here tonight. Doc has the distinction of being the only student ever to pull a prank on Mr. Anderson, and everyone expects to hear that story tonight.

Ted Stone was the head football coach for 17 years. People say he touched more lives than any teacher in the history of the school district. Jay Hawkins will be here tonight to tell the story of how Ted saved his life—"Kept me out of jail or worse," Jay tells anyone who will listen. No one really liked Ted when they were in school. His players called him "Sir" and often threatened to quit halfway through the season. But who was going to quit a team that always made the play-offs, even if they only won the championship nine of Ted's 17 years as head coach? Ted always said he won football games because he understood kids and because he would take players that most teachers didn't want in their classrooms and turn them into stars. If you played football for Ted Stone, you were either a tutor or a person being tutored, because Ted "didn't want illiterates on his team."

Finally, there is Sue. Only Mrs. Connor and a few students who were never in the chorus called her Miss Baldwin. Everyone else called her Sue. In fact, that is why Mrs. Connor stressed her formal title. She hated the fact that Sue allowed students to call her by her first name. Sue would tell her students to call her Miss Baldwin in the hall, but she loved being called by her first name. "My students respect me because I care about them, not because I am their teacher," Sue would tell Mrs. Connor. Her students did respect her, and loved her too. Most felt that they learned a lot about music from Sue, but they learned more about life and about being a quality human being. Sue's students won numerous music awards because they wanted to please her. Joy will tell the story tonight of her experience as a person "who still can't carry a tune" even though she was part of Sue's state chorus in her senior year.

What made these very different teachers stars? How did they touch so many lives in such different yet positive ways? What would you do if you had all of them in your school? Would you put them all on the same team? After all, collectively they are an ideal representation of the Four *P*s. When we speak of striking a balance in terms of the Four *P*s, do we really think that every team should be made up of an equal amount of Guardian, Artisan, Idealist, and Rational characteristics?

The Four *P* balance does not occur naturally in any school or school district. Schools are predominantly Guardian institutions because much of what we do involves passing on knowledge and the culture. Schools have a high percentage of Idealists because educators exist to make the next generation more successful than their own. Public schools are about the continuation of all that we are and all that we want to become. We send our children to schools, and we want them to be in stable, caring environments. But we also value risk taking and exploration. Let's look at the dilemma that these competing interests pose for public schools, and consider how we can shift people's attitudes from seeing differences as competing values to seeing them as significant pieces of what can become quality schools.

Your stakeholders can develop a more balanced approach to the Four *P*s. But most people are more comfortable doing the things they enjoy than they are doing the things that other people expect of them. How can you manage tasks in ways that allow your stakeholders to do the things they do well and trust other stakeholders to do the rest?

Your stakeholders will give you the benefit of the doubt when they believe that you value their contributions, and will follow you when you help them realize their expectations. Find success and replicate it. Take a look at the following skills required to manage tasks and lead people:

- Understanding personality differences
- Understanding the skills required to complete a task
- Matching people's talents with the needs of the task at hand
- Providing equal access to information
- Coordinating tasks to focus stakeholders' efforts toward a shared purpose

We have already discussed personality differences. Let's shift our focus to the task analysis.

Conducting a Task Analysis

If you want your stakeholders to be responsible for student learning, their roles and responsibilities should be based on their expertise and interests rather than on politics. You can use the task analysis checklist that appears in Figure 5.2 as a first step toward matching school district tasks with stakeholders' talents.

Your stakeholders can use the task analysis checklist as they formulate their critical Four *P* questions. They can derive tasks and subtasks from your strategic goals. Stakeholders should ask what *goal* is driving the need for a task and what specific *charge* should guide the work of the task force. They should understand clear lines of *authority,* including

	FIGURE 5.2
	Task Analysis Checklist
Goals	Which of the strategic plan goals does this task address?
Task	What is the specific charge that guides this task force?
Authority	Who empowered the task force and to whom does it report?
Critical Questions	What are the critical questions that guide the work of this task force?
Coordination	Who is responsible for coordinating the work of the task force?
Participation	What stakeholder groups should participate on the task force, and what voice will they have in decision making?
Expectations	What products or reports should result from the work of this group?
Time Lines	What is the timeline for this group, including start-up, phasing, interim reports, and final delivery of products and reports?

- Who authorized the task (school board, superintendent, curriculum committee, etc.).
- The *critical questions* they have been asked to answer.
- Who is responsible for *coordinating* the group and the task.
- Who can or should expect to participate in the task force, and how they are to be selected/elected.
- The *expectations* for conducting business and reporting actions.
- The *timelines* under which they are to operate.

Whether on a district level or on a building level, individuals need to think critically about why a task is important. Again, Keirsey and Bates's research (1998) indicates that less than 10 percent of people turn automatically to rational thinking as a way to solve problems. Forty-five to 50 percent of people (Guardians) approach problem solving from a perspective of "doing what they do better." Another 35 to 40 percent experiment until something works. The extent to which you match stakeholders' talents with their roles and responsibilities for a task can help to determine how much effort they are willing to contribute toward that task. If you can match tasks with stakeholders' interests and talents, a task force is more likely to function as a team. This is what it means to reframe the organizational purpose as opposed to reinventing it.

Influencing Success Without Dictating the Solution

Your leadership depends more on influence than on authority. You can require temporary behavior changes from stakeholders, but you will need their cooperation if you want them to form the Four *P* habits. A task force's success depends on a clear focus and effective facilitation. As stakeholders learn to conduct ongoing tasks in ways that promote success for all students, the Four *P*s become more and more a part of the culture districtwide. Let's use the Thompson District's experience with middle-level education to demonstrate how important a task analysis can be.

The Thompson School Board acted in 1989 to move from a junior high (grades 7–9) structure to a middle school alignment of grades 6, 7, and 8. To its credit, the school board recognized that such a shift meant more than changing grade-level configurations; it required a major shift in thinking about the education of middle-level students. But Thompson leaders only did what habit told them they should do. They "told" people what product they wanted and "invited" the staff to create a middle school. This Guardian assignment, coupled with an Idealist sense of involvement, was a good start, but it simply did not go far enough. The lack of trust that emerged from this task over a 12-year period (and the very fact that it lasted 12 years) can be traced to a number of missing links from the task analysis checklist:

1. The school board and administration did not provide specific charges outlining the responsibilities of the group relative to the district's

strategic goals. This lack of precision led to confusion, wasted time, and ultimately a lack of trust.

2. The school board and administration failed to ensure that all group members had equal access to information. The task also lacked specific time lines.

3. The school board and administration failed to outline the relationship of the task force to other groups within the school and district—groups to whom they were responsible or that were responsible to them. It was simply not clear who was responsible for what and what would happen to the group's work once it was completed.

4. The school board and administration failed to stipulate the critical questions to be investigated. Paul and Elder (2002) point out that a significant part of any critical analysis is knowing the question to be answered.

5. The school board and administration failed to provide criteria that would define an effective solution to problems. No one inside or outside the group could determine whether or not a proposed solution had been achieved in a fair and appropriate manner.

6. The school board and administration failed to suggest group protocols and task structures that would promote critical thinking and creativity. Therefore, the group's work soon became a process of "sharing ignorance."

7. The school board and administration failed to specify the product that was to result from the work of the task force. After years of research, discussion, and political maneuvering, all that the district had to show for its work was a general sense of disappointment and an incredible lack of trust.

When a fourth task force concluded its work in 2003, the Thompson school board recognized the lack of direction and what it termed "poor communications." Remember, at its best, quality is a shifting target. When people fail to paint a target at the beginning of a task, quality depends totally on chance. Your stakeholders can change their behaviors quickly if you ask them to do so. To change their habits requires a clear target, preferably one that they help to create.

Matching Tasks and Talents

As you evolve through the five steps toward quality schools, expect to be criticized for not living up to your own expectations. As Dolan (1994) indicates, it is impossible to stop the operations of a school district in order to introduce a "new and improved" program or service. Children arrive at the schoolhouse door every day whether or not the staff is ready for them. Teachers retire every year, taking with them a history of understanding and relationships and creating a different set of dynamics for the teams they leave behind. Each year, children move from one school to another, taking their parents with them and creating a void in the parent history on the site accountability advisory committee. New state and federal regulations can alter or even negate years of work and careful planning.

Even with an effective task analysis, your stakeholders need ongoing clarification and support. Bridges (1991) suggests that leaders should be prepared to repeat information over and over and to provide training and support so that stakeholders can develop new skills. You need to build the capacity of your stakeholders. They may not be able to master every skill they need to complete a task successfully, but they can recognize when another skill—one that is not necessarily their strong suit—is required. This is when they will come to appreciate differences and depend on one another to reach a common goal.

A good way to develop balance in your school district is to familiarize your stakeholders with the Four *P*s. There are numerous instruments you can use to help them understand personality differences (see National Curriculum and Training Institute, 1995). Can your stakeholders recognize and appreciate their own Four *P* tendencies? Do they recognize the aspect of each task where their strengths can come into play? If they are not particularly capable of risk taking, can they step back and allow others to negotiate those areas, or do they allow their fear of the unknown to limit their ability to move forward?

People who can apply Rational skills and assume some degree of risk (Artisan skills) can be quite effective in inventing a new program or strategy, but they may need to call on their Guardian colleagues to organize and manage the logistical aspects of the task. And if these "rational risk takers" don't learn to exercise their Guardian and Idealistic talents to some degree, other stakeholders may begin to view them as manipulative or opportunistic: "He always has to be the star," "He doesn't really care about kids," or "It's always about numbers with him."

There are two fundamental factors that affect the Four P balance on committees and task forces: stakeholders' understanding of their own Four P tendencies, and their acceptance of other people's Four P tendencies. How effectively do you support this balance on your committees and task forces? Hiebert and colleagues (1997) suggest several core features of a "safe" classroom environment. Figure 5.3 is an adaptation of these ideas for use with a committee or task force. Have you created a safe environment for your stakeholders to share ideas?

Kyle's experience with his middle school staff provides a good example of creating a balanced environment for a task force, especially when it comes to leaving behind something of value. Kyle had several teachers at his school who seemed to take a negative view of most task force reports. Therefore, he kept most task force topics simple, thinking that small successes would build his staff's confidence and encourage them to move toward bigger issues over time. One teacher finally told Kyle that the staff resented spending so much time on trivial issues. They had begun to feel manipulated.

Kyle engaged a task force in the study of pre–advanced placement (AP) strategies for middle school math and was pleasantly surprised by the outcome. Rather than trying to control the normally negative voices from the group, Kyle asked one of them, Christine, to chair the task force. He provided clear guidelines for the group's work and led the members to several resources on pre-AP studies. He helped them establish group norms for their work and

FIGURE 5.3
Developing a Balanced Learning Environment

Dimension		Core Feature
Creating a clear focus	⟶	Identify a real problem that leaves behind something of value.
Equity and accessibility	⟶	Provide access to all stakeholder groups and opportunities for every member to contribute and be heard.
Clarifying roles	⟶	Review task analysis together.
Tools	⟶	Engage in research; allow group to determine method, format, and frequency of meetings and communication.
Meeting cultural expectations	⟶	Share ideas and information openly, view mistakes as chances to learn, evaluate progress according to criteria.

Source: Adapted from Hiebert et al. (1997).

scheduled time for them to meet as a group. Kyle was amazed to see the quality of work that emerged from the group and the extent to which a leadership role could change a negative voice into a contributing partner. Christine later confided to him that, as a Rational, she was often put off by all the "silly politics" of her Guardian colleagues. She had not realized how negative her assessments of other people's work had seemed. Placed in a leadership role, she was obliged to own both the problem and the solution. And she came to appreciate her colleagues' ability to organize information and create a manageable focus.

When parents and staff react favorably to different "personalities" over time, they model appropriate learning for students. People may appreciate an Artisan's sense of risk taking when it involves something other than students. Some may respond well to an Idealist's sensitivity in a social setting but consider them naive in task force situations. Others may value a Rational's objectivity in some situations but find them cold or impersonal.

As people solve problems together, they come to understand how certain circumstances require more or less of certain Four *P* skills. They realize that a teammate's failure to appreciate their contributions may be as much a factor of a negative situation as it is a judgment of ideas and their worth. (People tend to resist what they don't understand.) Your stakeholders can learn to appreciate another person's Four *P* tendencies without devaluing their own.

Don't assume that the Four *P*s are a separate phenomenon to be practiced and discussed in isolation. You can help your stakeholders gain a better understanding of the Four *P*s through personality inventories, but these alone are not enough to change a school culture. At Thompson, administrators and key teacher leaders also received training in Paul and Elder's (2002) eight elements of critical thinking. A Title I elementary school became a pilot site in the district for developing critical thinking skills and applying them on a schoolwide basis. Other schools used Marzano's (1988) dimensions of learning and Costa's (2001) research on developing minds as frameworks for teaching critical thinking skills. A task force of parents and staff developed a set of descriptors for a districtwide definition of critical thinking, and began an investigation of critical thinking assessment protocols. Several elementary staffs focused on infusing critical thinking into the existing mathematics curriculum.

The district's executive team and instructional directors received training in Hartzler and Henry's (1994) "Team Fitness Model," the school board received training in goal setting from the Colorado Association of School Boards, and numerous staff members used Holcomb's *Getting Excited About Data* (1999) and *Asking the Right Questions* (2001) to conduct staff and site accountability advisory committee discussions and planning sessions. All school board members, administrators, teacher association representatives, district accountability advisory committee members, and site accountability advisory chairs also received what the district referred to as a "Continuous Growth Access Notebook," which contained the following:

- Strategic plan
- Shared decision-making manual

- Accountability plan
- Long-range funding priorities plan
- District planning calendar
- Major district committee reporting structure and charges
- District organizational chart
- Yearly responsibility matrix

In 2003, the director of assessment met with all Thompson principals to help them analyze their student achievement data and set realistic goals for their yearly action plans. The district accountability advisory committee and several site accountability advisory committees invited the director to make presentations to their groups. The director also helped the elementary, middle, and high school principals prepare their midyear progress reports for the board of education.

But perhaps the most highly functioning team was at one of the district's middle schools. The team had demonstrated three consecutive years of significant growth across most student subgroups in reading and mathematics. When asked "Why have you been so successful as a team?" these middle school teachers responded that they had a shared purpose for learning; agreed on a common focus for yearly goals and unit goals; reflected on student growth, including analyses of curriculum units and teaching strategies; and held each other accountable.

A shared commitment can fade quickly when team members change or when the team experiences stress. It can fade even more quickly if you fail to define tasks clearly or train and support teams. Thompson leaders had to restart their change process because they had considered only two of the Four *P*s when they tried to implement the shift from junior high to middle school. The change process needed a Rational structure and a clear sense of what would happen when the work was complete (the Artisan commitment to make something happen).

School leaders took time to conduct refresher workshops for site administrators and site accountability advisory committee chairs. They used simulated problems involving curriculum, instructional delivery, goal setting, and discipline. Later, they also conducted abbreviated sessions with teachers' association leaders.

Patience and perseverance paid off in this situation. A year after the middle school review problems occurred, Thompson high schools experienced a similar challenge. But in that case, the process had begun with a focus on the task analysis checklist, using the parameters of districtwide protocols for planning, decision making, accountability, and funding priorities. It started with the question "What should students know and be able to do when they graduate from the Thompson School District?" While a handful of unhappy parents and staff questioned certain program decisions, leaders were able to keep stakeholders focused on mutually developed protocols and a clearly defined analysis of the task at hand. They were able to manage the conflict without a tremendous amount of personal attacks and without interrupting the review process.

It takes time to shift school improvement from what Peale (1974) calls the Three *L*s—lack, loss, and limitation—to an assets model of change. The shift will never occur unless you can keep your stakeholders connected and involved through a shared purpose. The people involved in decisions may vary from task to task, but the fundamental parameters for determining which stakeholder groups should be involved and how they should be involved should be consistent from the classroom to the boardroom. Be sure to keep stakeholders focused on the types of cooperative problem-solving attitudes and behaviors that they expect students to demonstrate in the classroom. You may also want your school board to develop a policy regarding various stakeholders' roles in planning, decision making, accountability, and funding priorities.

Do you want teachers to collaborate with parents and students to make classroom decisions about learning? Do you want groups of teachers to function collaboratively with parents and students to coordinate two or more sets of classroom learning experiences toward a shared purpose? If so, you must manage districtwide tasks to model the collaboration skills. You must make collaboration an organizational expectation. When you do, you will transform random acts of effectiveness into sustainable quality schools. Quality is a shifting target. Solutions to one problem often create new problems. But you can limit inconsistencies by creating site protocols that are consistent with districtwide protocols (strategic, shared decision making, accountability, and funding priorities plans). Let's examine how information flow affects coordination.

Coordinating Information Flow

Communication (or lack of communication) is often cited as a key factor in failed change attempts. Each year, you probably have task forces and committees that conduct investigations and make recommendations to the staff or the school board. These groups may suggest the implementation of programs and services based on their work. But how do you coordinate the work of one committee or task force with that of other groups? What happens when the staff or school board does not like a task force recommendation?

Roberts (2000) suggests that to lead a learning organization, you must be a learner-centered leader. You should demonstrate that you are not certain of the answers and that you find challenge in the unknown. You must recognize and help those around you recognize that often the ideal solution does not exist. In these situations, you must look for options rather than answers.

To avoid turning an options discussion into a power struggle, you may want to develop a flowchart showing how various task forces and committees relate to one another. The committee flowchart assists stakeholders in knowing with whom they need to collaborate to ensure that they are working consistently toward the same strategic goals. You can have each major district committee suggest areas the members have studied and where their research has taken them. Encourage them to suggest areas for future research and share their suggestions with the school board in the form of recommended committee charges. You may even want to create a committee flowchart, as illustrated in Figure 5.4. This is not an organizational chart; it merely indicates how major committees communicate with one another, where their information flows, and who is responsible for communicating recommendations to the school board.

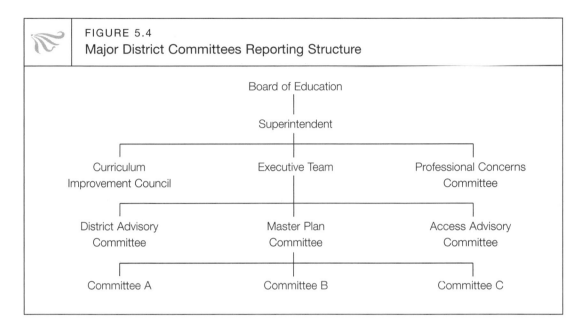

FIGURE 5.4
Major District Committees Reporting Structure

Board of Education

Superintendent

Curriculum Improvement Council   Executive Team   Professional Concerns Committee

District Advisory Committee   Master Plan Committee   Access Advisory Committee

Committee A   Committee B   Committee C

The exact nature of your committee chart is not important. What is important is removing ambiguities and encouraging partnerships. Negroni (2000) points out that isolating opposition or controlling appointments merely encourages opposition. Negroni, a Massachusetts superintendent, says leaders do not need to give up their own principles to understand someone else's. The purpose of committees and task forces is to improve communication, not to control it. The reporting chart helps committees organize their work, share information, and cooperate in as many ways as possible to achieve the district's strategic goals.

After your school board officially adopts committee charges, the real work begins. It would be just as foolhardy for educators to think that all risks can be avoided as it would be to act in haste. Growth implies some degree of risk, but risks can be mitigated if your stakeholders develop the habit of reflecting-in-action—that is, monitoring and adjusting their work as changes evolve. Your job is to ensure that they gather information fairly and report it consistently from the classroom to the boardroom.

Committees, task forces, and teams can operate simultaneously to gather and analyze research, map and revise curriculum, integrate instructional strategies across content areas, plan lessons and units, and so on. It is important that educators know the purpose and scope of their task, the parameters for including other stakeholders appropriately within and across tasks, and how to share information between and among all stakeholder groups. Tasks should be identified, along with the leaders responsible for coordinating each task, the priorities considered, and the strategic goals addressed by the programs or services under consideration.

Many school districts are effective at reporting to people when they want their support. You may even be very effective at asking for your stakeholders' input. Where many leaders fall short, however, is in communicating the results of their work. Your stakeholders will understand that tasks can take longer than initially planned. Just be certain to give them periodic progress reports. Aside from a required yearly report, Thompson schools send monthly school board agendas and superintendent memos to all site accountability advisory committee chairs. They send a quarterly electronic newsletter to all district committee members, and they encourage stakeholders to sign up for the electronic newsletter at parent conferences and open houses. Your communications can be brief, but at a minimum should include information about the following:

- Program or service name
- Descriptions of how the program or service addresses strategic goals
- What the program or service costs in staff, time, and dollars
- When you had initially expected to complete it, how much progress you have made, and the new expected completion date

That information demonstrates the benefits of shared decision making tied to strategic goals. It shifts stakeholders' thinking from political action to the development of a body of evidence—success for whom, under what conditions, given what evidence. At first, your stakeholders may want to control information flow. They may say, "Let's get our own act together before we share this information with the community." Or you may hear, "I don't think most parents are really interested in all the details. Let's just put the information into a newsletter. Then we can meet with parents when we have some of the bugs worked out." What this approach neglects is having parents bear witness to the struggle that underlies educational decisions.

Your stakeholders know that your school district will not have adequate funds to address all recommendations emerging from committees and task forces. But when they take part in the process and receive progress reports, they know where their recommendations stand relative to other district priorities. You can use your school district's funding priorities plan as more than a budgeting document; it can be a communication tool for keeping track of committee and task force recommendations. It can report how those recommendations were analyzed and where they fall relative to other school district priorities.

Reports and summaries do not need to be lengthy, complicated documents. For any document more than five pages long, you may also want to provide an executive summary. You can have raw data and background analyses available, but remember that your stakeholders are busy people. Parents have jobs of their own, and staff members who serve on committees have classroom teaching responsibilities. Wherever possible, use summaries or checklists. Figure 5.5 illustrates a few examples of the kinds of information you might report.

Your school board can discuss these reports publicly and share them with district committees. They can ask questions and obtain additional staff and community input at public meetings and then use a form similar to the one illustrated in Figure 5.6 to set funding priorities. The school board members should each review the information in the first four columns, then individually indicate how they would like to allocate available dollars among the recommended priorities. The final column should be used to compare board members' preferences.

When the school board shares information and makes decisions publicly, people learn to trust the system. They come to accept that they can

FIGURE 5.5
Sample Summary Report

Strategic Plan Goal Areas	Key Areas of Focus for 2002–2003
General: Whole Child, Logistics, Underlying Principles	• Curriculum process completed and initial implementation begun • Implementation of Web-based communications with parents • Work toward middle school task force recommendations
Basic Skills: Literacy	• Elementary support of balanced literacy training • Secondary support and planning for reading and writing across content areas
Basic Skills: Math	• Training and support for new math curriculum • Training in problem-based math, including ongoing coaching • Literacy training in math
Critical Thinking and Creativity	• Communication and refining of definitions • Identification of assessments that are already in place and assessment needs

make a difference. When the school board values their participation and helps them recognize their expectations, they will value the school board's leadership.

Coordinating Tasks

You can make information more accessible by making tasks consistent across organizational structures. For example, the site equivalent to the strategic plan is the school effectiveness plan (see Chapter 3). Both should be similar in form and substance. Your site plans should drive district planning. However, plans are only as effective as the decision-making structures that support them. Principals in your school district need clear parameters for connecting the school effectiveness plan not only with the district's strategic plan but also with each grade level and department's planning and goal setting

FIGURE 5.6
Funding Priorities Review

	Budget Information			Board Member
Budget Priority	Rationale	Cost/FTE	Options 2003–2004	A B C D E F G
Funding for educational options— mixed levels	Meet the needs of diverse learners: • Summer transition program between levels • Credit Recovery Program offered at night during the year to . . .	• $40,000 for secondary Jump Start • $35,000 for Credit Recovery Program • Costs of both programs tied mainly to teachers' salaries	• Jump Start and Credit Recovery Program could become optional • $20,000 would allow us to run the 8th and 9th grade programs for . . .	

process, as well as with each teacher's yearly planning and goal-setting strategies. Individual teachers and grade level and department teams, in turn, can connect their unit and lesson planning to the effectiveness plan.

Every school in the Thompson system has its own shared decision-making manual that is aligned with the one produced by the district. Thompson teachers and administrators resisted this alignment at first, thinking it would be too confining and make them all "cookie-cutter" schools. Eventually, they realized that coordination saved time and improved their ability to leverage resources. Three Title I elementary school principals found that they could use their plans as a springboard to create not only monthly planning and professional development meetings for themselves but also common professional development activities for their staffs.

You can coordinate tasks from school to school and from one level to another if you manage the planning cycle effectively. When schools follow a similar planning and analysis time line, they can reflect and collaborate on multiple levels within and across school sites. Thompson leaders use the cycle illustrated in Figure 5.7 to coordinate their planning districtwide. Think about how you could adapt this cycle to meet needs within your school district. Consider the rules and regulations that you already have in place, as well as your stakeholders' individual and group talents. As Goodlad (2004) suggests, don't reform your schools, renew them. Renew a sense of empowerment that individual stakeholders can make a difference. Look at the sample planning cycle in Figure 5.7. Keep in mind that it's not the specific time line but consistency and focus on success that are important.

Once people get into the habit of planning toward a shared focus, you can begin to elevate their reflection from a compliance review to a qualitative analysis process. They will be able to reframe school district goals and

FIGURE 5.7 Planning Cycle	
Tasks Performed on a Yearly Basis	
Summer	District organizes student data for each site.
Fall	Sites analyze data and set local goals consistent with district goals, completing action plan in the form of a school effectiveness plan similar to the responsibility matrix.
Fall	District reviews site plans for trends by level and creates plan to support site plans.
January	Progress is reported at midyear and is used to project budget needs for the ensuing year according to a district responsibility matrix that supports common needs by level.
Summer	Evidence, in the form of assessments and surveys, is collated.
Fall	Sites report progress from previous year and create new action plans.

underlying principles so that their day-to-day tasks are linked to their long-term strategies. Thompson principals created a common scoring rubric, shown in Figure 5.8, that helped them focus change efforts across the district. The rubric helps to identify traits of proposals that qualify the proposals as exemplary, satisfactory, in need of improvement, or unacceptable. It was developed through a series of meetings with principals and district office administrators. You can use a similar rubric to manage tasks throughout your schools. It provides focus without inhibiting flexibility for each staff to meet the unique needs of their students.

You can use a rubric to provide feedback to site staff and advisory committees and to provide evidence to the district accountability advisory committee that the accountability process is encouraging qualitative review and coordination of a shared district purpose. Other attributes and criteria you might wish to consider include the following:

- Data analysis reflected in goals, tasks, and strategies
- Focus shown in goals, tasks, and strategies
- Congruence and logic of goals, tasks, and strategies
- Use of professional development resources
- Integration of technology and media services
- High and achievable basic skills goals

FIGURE 5.8
School Effectiveness Plan Rubric

Attribute/ Criteria	Exemplary	Satisfactory	Needs Improvement	Unacceptable/ Must Be Revised
Alignment with strategic goals	Goal is clearly aligned with and supports the district's strategic goals.	Goal is aligned with the district's strategic goals.	Goal is not clearly aligned with the district's strategic goals.	Goal does not align with the strategic plan.

- Adequate yearly progress in closing the achievement gap for subgroup populations
- Growth for *all* students

Managing tasks is a key step toward leading people. Effective leaders must be effective managers. Just remember that you need to manage tasks and lead people. Given the right critical questions and the appropriate management protocols, stakeholders can assume responsibility for *strategic thinking* that translates individual beliefs about students and learning into a clearly articulated organizational *purpose*. A shared purpose cuts across all organizational structures to create organizational *parameters* through which learning and teaching decisions are made, from the classroom to the boardroom. It encourages *personal accountability* for organizational *principles* that make programs and services accessible to all stakeholders. When you manage tasks and information flow effectively, you can *leverage resources* toward organizational *priorities*.

Quality Through Renewal

Success breeds success, but it also elevates expectations. When your stakeholders see that they can have a positive effect on student achievement and well-being, they will not be satisfied with the status quo. In *Romances with Schools* (2004), Goodlad speaks of carrying on an intimate relationship with education. He suggests that school reform is foisted upon unwilling teachers and administrators, while school renewal is created with their willing participation.

The Guardians who make up 60 to 70 percent of your school district won't change by force. But neither will they change without encouragement and support. The key to sustainable change in any school district lies in intimacy. Each student, parent, teacher, administrator, and school board member must become intimately engaged with learning. We feel safe with those whom we know intimately; we feel committed to them, and we overlook their flaws in order to see the good in them and to gain the greatest benefit for ourselves.

As in a marriage, the intimacy involved with school renewal is not always found in someone who is just like us. More often, it is found in someone who completes us. Lasting intimacy comes with a complete disclosure of information. It necessitates taking shared responsibility for successes and setbacks rather than ascribing blame. You need to be honest and sensitive to other people's needs and caring enough to plan for the future together. You need to struggle in the face of impossible odds together and stay focused on a common purpose that is greater than any one participant. As Goodlad (2004) suggests, intimacy lies in a common purpose that is so deeply ingrained in the school's psyche that it permeates all daily activities.

Intimacy is hard to create in a large group. Consider applying the following suggestions to your situation:

- Start planning at the school site and let it ripple from group to group
- Coordinate site goals into the overall strategic goals of the school district
- Establish clear targets across classrooms, grades, and departments
- Conduct task analyses to align purpose and practice
- Define the relationships between and among major district committees
- Expect stakeholders to become intimately aware of these groups and how they contribute to and are personally accountable for student achievement and well-being

The key to quality is to search for what works as opposed to what stakeholders think does not work. Success should be measured in terms of student achievement and well-being, and it should be measured across all student groups.

As the Third International Mathematics and Science Study research indicates, expectations are highly correlated with performance (Kroeze & Johnson, 1997). Teachers need to develop a collaborative effort with students and parents in order to nurture and sustain learning. This need for collaboration becomes even more complex as tasks emerge across grades and departments, school sites, levels, and the district as a whole.

Change is not about a single program or strategy. The magic lies in the connections that you and your stakeholders build between and among your aims and strategies. But these connections cannot be sustained without a structure that encourages an intimate relationship among all learners.

Again, quality is as much a factor of values as it is of standards. No matter what standards the public schools achieve, their quality depends on how much people value what they produce. The more consistently people meet one another's expectations over time and across groups and communities, the closer they will come to achieving and sustaining quality schools. The more individuals see themselves as intimately involved with meeting expectations, the more willing they will be to assume accountability for their actions.

In the final chapter, we will examine the demands that expectations for quality schools place on leaders and discuss how you can make leadership positions more attractive in your school district. But first, ask yourself how close you and your stakeholders are to closing the gap between purpose and practice in your district by answering the following questions:

1. How are strategic goals, a written decision-making process, an accountability and action planning process, and a long-range funding priorities plan connected in your community?
2. Do all stakeholders share responsibility for coordinating those processes at all levels?
3. What tasks have emerged from the strategic plan in your school or district?
4. Write down how many of the elements from the task analysis checklist were included in planning for each of the tasks in question 1.
5. What other projects or processes already under way in the district might interfere with or need to be coordinated with your strategic goals?

6. Do funding priorities in your school or district drive budget decisions?

7. List specific preparation and implementation plans for closing the gap between purpose and practice under the following steps:

- *Step 1:* Discussing the task analysis checklist with stakeholders
- *Step 2:* Creating a school or district committee/task force reporting structure, including yearly charges
- *Step 3:* Finding success and replicating it
- *Step 4:* Piloting a funding priorities process

6

Nurturing Balanced Leadership

Lead, follow, and *get out of the way.*

What does the quality target look like in your school district? How do you see it? How do your stakeholders see it? Are you a balanced leader who knows how to engage your stakeholders in tasks that achieve a shared purpose? Do your stakeholders know the rules of the game in your school culture? Do they hold themselves accountable for success? Do task forces and committees in your school district accomplish something meaningful and leave something of value behind? Remember, you will never fully attain quality; it is an elusive target that moves every time you seem to be within reach. It is not as important that you hit the target every time as it is that you and your community agree on what the target is. People who are engaged in defining the quality target and in deciding when to move it know just how difficult it is to hit it consistently over time. Leadership is about helping stakeholders make those decisions in ways that promote achievement and well-being for *all* students.

Change in a public school environment is more about evolution than revolution. Goodlad and colleagues (2004) suggest that it is also more about renewal than reform. Reform is about pushing change from the outside.

Reformers see the data on student achievement as an indication that public schools cannot educate students for today's world, and want to reorganize or replace the schools with something better. Those who would renew public schools from within suggest that schools are merely a reflection of the communities that they serve. They suggest that change inside the school walls cannot be sustained without changing expectations outside those walls—changing the attitudes and perceptions of the community about what constitutes an educated person and how that goal can be achieved.

In recalling his experiences with Madeline Hunter at the University of California at Los Angeles lab school, Goodlad (2004) speaks of their combined concern for both pedagogy and culture. In those recollections, Goodlad recognizes a need to prepare a school culture for a change in thinking. He identifies a problem-solving sequence that includes dialogue about the problem, decisions regarding a course of action, implementation or action, and evaluation. To achieve this kind of thinking, stakeholders must be intimately involved in the process. Leaders, in turn, must provide an organizational structure that promotes and supports learning at all levels.

I am often struck by the repeated message from parents and educators that everything they do is "for the kids." Yet when they are asked what benefit kids will gain from what adults are doing, they often speak of skills that will be useful in adulthood. This message of "work now and reap the benefits later" comes as no surprise when you know that 60 to 70 percent of a school staff is composed of Guardians. But what does this attitude offer to the Artisans who make up 40 to 45 percent of the student population? If we fail to make learning fun now, how can we expect to achieve our goal of creating lifelong learners?

As I listened recently to children reading letters of appreciation to their favorite teachers, I was taken both by what they did and did not say. First, every single child in the group of 20 to 30 students cited the teachers' ability to connect—to see something of merit in the student that other adults (and in many cases, the child) had missed. At the same time, not one child thanked a teacher for improving test scores.

In *Teachers with Class* (2003), Goldberg and Feldman share strikingly similar stories from famous Americans. James Earl Jones thanks his teacher Mr. Crouch for using poetry to overcome his stuttering. Walter Cronkite thanks Fred Birney for teaching him journalism, but more importantly for what he taught him about the responsibilities of being a journalist: "You've got to remember that everyone you write about is a human being," he said. Cindy Crawford thanks Mr. Halvorson for "filling his students with excitement and anticipation for the future."

As these tributes attest, children learn more from modeling than from any other instructional strategy. Schools today have become joyless places—places where the incentive for learning has become a test score. But is the solution to replace the schools or to redirect them?

Mark is one of the finest instructional minds in the educational profession. With an undergraduate degree in special education and a doctorate from Vanderbilt, he served as a middle school principal, assistant superintendent, and superintendent before leaving the profession in frustration. Mark's major obstacle as a school leader is that he is an Artisan in a Guardian world. But after working two years in the charter school arena, Mark has concluded that the challenge is not in the pace of change but in its depth. Unless school leaders change people's attitudes about the purpose of schooling, reforms will come and go at an increasingly rapid pace.

As an example of this "fix it fast" mentality, consider the yearly legislative changes in state after state with laws (all designed to fix education) actually counteracting one another. In Colorado, K–12 education has been pitted against all other state departments because of two constitutional amendments: one that limits the state's ability to raise taxes and one that requires it to spend more and more dollars on education.

What we need is balance—a balance that matches the personality of the school environment with the personality of the community. Schools are by their very nature Guardian institutions whose major responsibility is to pass on the culture and to promote democratic ideals. But democracy is not static; at its finest, democracy requires critical thinking and knowledgeable participation, as well as an understanding of what it means to be free to make choices and what it means to be held accountable for those choices. Students must learn basic skills, but those skills are useless without an understanding of how to apply them toward the common good. And who will practice what they cannot enjoy?

The Role of Leaders in Achieving Balance

Because success breeds success, effective school leaders must be able to provide multiple pathways for all stakeholders to become successful. Senge and colleagues (2000) suggest the following five skills necessary to providing these pathways (followed by a brief definition within the context of this book):

- Personal mastery—articulating your own coherent vision for schools
- Shared vision—creating a common purpose
- Mental models—developing reflection and inquiry skills
- Team learning—conducting dialogue and skillful discussions
- Systems thinking—understanding the interdependence of schools and communities

The first step in modeling balanced leadership is to understand your leadership strengths and liabilities. If you are a school leader, the chances are seven in 10 that you are a Guardian. You have probably memorized the five steps outlined in this book. But do you understand their purpose and how they are connected? Can you use them in your own day-to-day practice? Can you help other people to use them effectively? More important, do you believe that your stakeholders have something to contribute toward quality schools? If not, you will find it difficult to sustain quality over time and across groups and communities.

Don't despair. You are not alone in your struggle to turn a meaningful purpose into effective, sustainable practice. Leaders, like everyone else, have learned to think about and interact with the world in ways that feel comfortable to them and to us. After a while, we lose sight of other ways of thinking, choosing friends and employees whose values and beliefs mesh with our own. In time, these choices become habits. Unfortunately, these habits (often called leadership styles) can limit leadership opportunities and limit the effectiveness of a school district.

For example, Robert can walk into an administrative meeting dressed as Carnac the Magnificent and for the next 10 minutes keep 40 principals and program directors in stitches. By the end of that meeting, he will have engaged three or more principals in sharing a skill or technique, four to five directors in facilitating small-group activities, and every participant in modeling a new skill or strategy. Robert knows how to initiate a conversation, play a support role for other administrators, and get out of people's way so that they can experience leadership and learning roles firsthand. But not everyone can be a Robert.

Like school districts, leaders are to a great extent a product of their culture. We are influenced by personal experiences, by our stakeholders' expectations, and by the traditional views of our profession. However, to an even greater extent, we are driven by our personal temperament—the way we see the world.

If we ignore our temperament, it will get in our way. But if we recognize its strengths and learn to rely on others to make up for its liabilities, we will find the balance we need to become effective leaders. Let's take a moment to review the five steps described in the previous chapters in order to explore ways of nurturing balanced leadership in your school district.

Leadership as a Function of Personality

Figure 6.1 contrasts the characteristics of the four leadership styles. These examples begin with a comparison of Guardians and Artisans, because they make up 75 to 85 percent of the general population. These are your concrete, results-oriented stakeholders. The Idealists and Rationals, who make up 15 to 25 percent of the population, are process-oriented individuals. What are the

FIGURE 6.1
Practical Leadership Comparisons

Guardians vs. Artisans

- Guardians know "that," while Artisans wonder "if."
- Guardians need to find, while Artisans hope to discover.
- Guardians try to protect, while Artisans try to win.
- Guardians want to collect the best, while Artisans want to collect many.
- Guardians seek the safest, while Artisans seek the fastest.

Idealists vs. Rationals

- Idealists need to feel, while Rationals need to understand why.
- Idealists love to talk with friends, while Rationals need time alone to think.
- Idealists enjoy a glass of wine, a good friend, and a warm fire, while Rationals enjoy a glass of wine, a good puzzle, and symphonic music.

implications for balanced leadership if 65 to 70 percent of your leaders are Guardians?

Purpose-Focused Leadership

Joe was an effective middle school principal. His staff loved him, his students loved him, and his students' parents loved him. Everyone loved Joe, who had been hired with great fanfare. He was a breath of fresh air following his predecessor's 17 years of stable but uneventful leadership.

Joe spent the first several months in his new position listening to parents and staff and interacting with students everywhere, such as in the lunchroom and during after-school activities. Joe accepted new ideas, and he found something positive to say about everyone. But by the end of the third quarter, people had begun to notice that nothing other than the atmosphere had changed—and that even the changes in atmosphere were not all positive. Student discipline was lax, parents were interfering with curriculum and instructional decisions, and staff members were bickering over leadership and direction across departments.

Joe was an Idealist—strong in terms of purpose and human relations but weak in terms of organization and problem solving. He was child centered, had a positive vision of what education could be, and wasn't afraid to take risks. But he couldn't make the tough decisions, and in fact avoided controversy at all costs. Joe's answer to controversy was to appoint a study committee. He was certain that "talented, caring people" could eventually come to consensus once they understood one another's perspectives. Joe even convinced the superintendent to pay for team building for his staff and parent advisory committee. But after two years of falling test scores and increasing discipline problems, Joe's hopes and the hopes of his parents and staff had not been realized.

Parameters-Focused Leadership

Lisa was a veteran elementary principal. Her staff depended on her to provide effective discipline, run effective staff meetings, stretch the school's budget, and protect teachers from the whims of parents and the district office. But Lisa's staff members did not find her particularly inspirational; in fact, they criticized her "obsessive" adherence to rules and regulations and her unwillingness to take chances. Lisa's teachers felt more safe than motivated, more protected than appreciated. Although Lisa hosted a staff party at her home every year, she discouraged impromptu celebrations at school.

Parents appreciated Lisa's consistent discipline, but they chafed at her unwillingness to support new ideas. They somewhat affectionately referred to her as "Low-Key Lisa." The students respected her but usually greeted her from a distance. They only expected to see her on the playground when there was a problem—except for once a year when she played in the staff-versus-5th-grade softball game.

Like 65 to 70 percent of her administrative peers, Lisa was a Guardian—clear on management parameters and expectations but weak in terms of people skills and innovation. She was effective at analyzing student achievement and always followed her students' academic and leadership achievements at the middle school level. She never missed an opportunity to highlight her school's alumni on the "Wall of Fame" just inside the front entrance to her school. This wall contained updated pictures of former students who were winning spelling bees, excelling in knowledge bowl competitions, and presiding over the student government or the honor society. The wall also contained a 10-year history of honor students by percentage of the middle school's population. And while their pictures weren't on the wall, Lisa could name numerous valedictorians, National Merit Scholars, and other high achievers who got their start in her school.

Lisa's parents and staff were proud of the school's accomplishments, but they worried about the students whose parents didn't get involved in school activities. They fought the district office for smaller class sizes and more counselors. They scheduled open houses and skating parties, but only the "good" parents seemed to get involved. They sent positive notes to every child's parents at least once during every school year. They knew that Lisa was giving it her all, but they were not surprised that many of their former students were dropping out of high school. After all, they had experienced a tremendous change in their student demographics.

Principles-Focused Leadership

Pete was a high school principal who had an amazing process for tracking student growth from 9th grade through postsecondary achievements. He had charts on state test scores by standard and subscale across all student subgroups, and had implemented before- and after-school tutoring programs with money he had obtained through competitive grants. Pete praised his teachers for their hard work, and he encouraged them to explore new ways to meet the needs of at-risk students. He had several committees analyzing test scores, participation in cocurricular activities, and dropout rates. Several other committees were investigating International Baccalaureate programs for high-achieving students, evening school, and online classes.

Unfortunately, Pete's staff members were exhausted. They appreciated Pete's enthusiasm and his belief that all students can learn, his willingness to work hard and to take risks, and his undying support of their efforts even when they failed to live up to his expectations. But it seemed that the more the teachers did, the more the parents and Pete expected them to do.

For the most part, parents supported Pete and appreciated his visionary leadership. But they wondered when he was going to "bring the hammer down" on staff members who were not pulling their weight. Praise, recognition, and hard work were all well and good, but parents and some members of the district office staff wanted Pete to hold his teachers more accountable for results. They also wanted to see Pete at more events—not just student events, but community events. They felt he was delegating too much to his assistants. They appreciated his focus on academics and his recognition of all student activities, but the football team had not won a championship in seven years. The basketball team had won the semifinals, but lost the championship to a high school that had put more time and money into year-round training and a new weight-training facility. They suggested that Pete should gather statistics on wins and losses and the effects of lost championships on the college prospects of student athletes.

Pete was a Rational—he studied hard, preferred computer spreadsheets to novels, and dreaded the inane conversations at community events. He hated whining, loathed excuses, and believed that failures were just interesting problems begging to be solved.

Priorities-Focused Leadership

Janet was a district office administrator, and unlike many of her peers, she was a risk taker. Janet would rather make a mistake and fix it than sit idly by waiting for something to work out or someone to give her permission. Staff appreciated her follow-through and admired her ability to juggle numerous tasks simultaneously—multitasking, she liked to call it.

Janet had received several state awards for her work on legislative issues and was well recognized among her peers on a national level. The superintendent and the school board relied heavily on her advice in teacher negotiations. They appreciated her fresh approach to issues and her prompt response to requests for information. She used her experience in the corporate world to her advantage in community meetings, avoiding educational jargon and speaking plainly to business leaders. Janet had made a meteoric rise in her newly adopted profession by negotiating favorable vendor contracts, balancing the budget, and running a lean but effective division for the school district.

Janet was an Artisan—practical, productive, and always looking for the next challenge. She gave people plenty of autonomy, but she sometimes failed to provide adequate supervision and support. Her veteran staff appreciated her faith in their ability, and they overlooked her little tirades when things did not go according to plans. They learned to live with the last-minute rush or the sudden change in direction. "That's just Janet," they would tell colleagues from other departments. However, some of Janet's peers and principals saw her as terse and flippant at times. They complained that she didn't understand the way things were done in a school environment. The few parents who had to deal with Janet about school issues often referred to her as brash or naive. New employees, particularly middle-level managers, complained that Janet was condescending and controlling. They noted her lack of clarity and her sudden changes in direction.

Connected Leadership

Joe, Lisa, Pete, and Janet were all effective leaders in many respects. Yet no matter what standards leaders achieve, their success depends on how much people value what they produce at any given moment. Quality is a moving target. Once attained, it becomes the standard, and people expect more—or if not more, at least something different.

Few leaders can meet people's expectations consistently over time. But successful leaders understand their own strengths and liabilities as they relate to the people around them. They use individual differences as a means of strengthening the long-term viability of the group. Let's examine how leaders can use the five steps described in this book to balance their own leadership and nurture balanced leadership in others.

Developing Balanced Leadership

It is important for leaders to model these five steps in their own leadership and to establish the same expectations across all organizational structures:

- Understanding the quality profile
- Asking quality questions
- Making quality a habit
- Focusing on success
- Managing tasks and leading people

Balanced leaders can use four districtwide tasks—strategic planning, shared decision making, accountability, and long-range funding prioritizing—to engage individuals and groups in the five steps outlined above:

- A *strategic planning process* focuses on people's values and beliefs about learning and teaching, and requires community stakeholders to ask why a program or strategy is important and how it contributes to students' learning and well-being.
- An effective *decision-making process* requires stakeholders to ask who should participate in various tasks and subtasks and in what capacities; it helps them determine the rules for moving the target.
- An effective *accountability process* requires stakeholders to hold themselves and one another accountable for using research data before, during, and after implementation of programs and services; stakeholders need to know which programs and services make a difference for which students under what circumstances.
- Effective *long-range funding prioritizing* requires stakeholders to leverage resources toward programs and services that work.

Figure 6.2 describes the leadership behaviors required to use those tools effectively.

FIGURE 6.2
Understanding and Applying the Five Steps

	Understanding the Five Steps	Applying the Five Steps
Step 1	Understand the Four Ps of leadership and management	Study and practice the Four Ps with stakeholders
Step 2	Ask the Four P questions and listen to people's answers	Use the Four Ps until they no longer seem awkward
Step 3	Establish districtwide protocols to make the Four Ps a habit	Give stakeholders the support they need to use the protocols consistently—explain, model, practice, and protect
Step 4	Expect everyone to be successful in achieving the Four Ps	Distinguish between personal comfort and organizational purpose
Step 5	Manage tasks and lead people	Vary organizational activities and assign tasks to suit people's talents

Studying and Practicing the Four Ps with Stakeholders

You can choose numerous personality inventories to use with your stakeholders. In addition to using the Myers-Briggs Type Indicator personality inventory (Myers, 1962), I have used the Real Colors inventory from the National Curriculum and Training Institute (NCTI, 1995) with school districts for almost 15 years.

NCTI uses four cards as a focal point for understanding the Four Ps. Although an effective facilitator can introduce the Real Colors exercise in a two-hour session, a half-day or even full-day introduction is more effective. The key is follow-up and practical application.

I like to introduce temperament concepts with school board members and administrators first so that they can model and support the concepts in their own settings. People tend to enjoy the workshops, and only a few skeptics worry about "labeling" others. I have found that people view personality inventories as intriguing but somewhat removed from reality.

In *The Real Colors Homeowner's Guide* (Johnson, 2004), I encourage people to take an inventory of the personality "stuff" that they've collected over the years. I ask them to complete an inventory by considering how their personal view of the world affects their day-to-day lives—how their beliefs, attitudes, and habits have become a part of who they are. You can use the inventory questions listed in Figure 6.3 to take an inventory of your own leadership characteristics.

Idealist leaders tend to focus primarily on purpose—connections among human beings and concepts that transcend physical or scientific explanations. Guardian leaders focus primarily on parameters—concrete, day-to-day objects and events and how they fit into manageable, predetermined categories. Rational leaders focus primarily on underlying principles—processes that connect ideas and principles to affect people's lives over time. Artisan leaders focus primarily on priorities—those concrete objects and events that are most readily available and hold the greatest potential to bring about immediate desired results.

FIGURE 6.3
Balanced Leadership Inventory

- Which of the Four *P*s (purpose, parameters, principles, priorities) do you emphasize most when you judge the effectiveness of a school program or service?
- In which of the Four *P* areas do you feel most comfortable or effective? In which do you feel least comfortable or effective?
- How consistent is your Four *P* order with the typical school order (parameters–purpose or purpose–parameters)?
- How has your own personality been an asset (or detriment) to your effectiveness as a school leader?
- How have you balanced or can you balance your leadership strengths with those of stakeholders to improve student achievement and well-being in your school?

Joyce, a Guardian and somewhat skeptical executive secretary, jokes that after thinking carefully about her temperament, she no longer knows what she believes. Then she adds, "This temperament stuff has made me question many of my assumptions." This is a great first step toward critical thinking. Joyce is extremely efficient and can become visibly agitated with people who do not follow directions—especially directions from the district office. She is sensitive and dedicated to making a difference for students, but she keeps people at arm's length. Like many Guardians, Joyce finds it easier to direct acquaintances (and chastise them if necessary) than to direct friends. The better we get to know people, the harder it becomes to direct them. If we are accountable for their performance, this intimacy can become a problem.

Using the Four *P*s Until They No Longer Seem Awkward

Remember that a liability is little more than a strength that we carry too far. Social misfits are likely to raise social misfits, and balanced adults are likely to raise balanced children, regardless of their Four *P* tendencies. But we can't pass on something we never owned. Teachers and parents seldom unleash their own Artisan and Rational tendencies at school. No matter how much they talk about critical thinking or risk taking, they seldom model these skills for children. Their actions also discourage these traits in school leaders.

Mark is an example of an effective leader who ran afoul of the Guardian culture in three school districts. When Mark was a middle school principal/special education director, students and parents loved his child advocacy approach to leadership: Mark expected staff to meet students' needs rather than shape students to fit existing school programs and routines.

Mark's staff members loved his sense of humor and appreciated his decisive approach to student discipline. But they resented the shifts in school routines (such as those that occurred when implementing curriculum differentiation) that he expected them to make to meet individual students' needs. Politically connected parents who had become accustomed to working through the Guardian culture also resented Mark's approach. They had come to expect special consideration because they were "involved" parents with "good" kids.

When Mark became an assistant superintendent in a wealthy suburban school district, he tried to tap his Guardian characteristics more effectively. He wore three-piece suits and replaced racquetball with golf. He cultivated powerful parents and staff. But when it came to getting the job done, Mark could not hide his Artisan nature. His success had been built on it.

Fortunately, in both those situations, Mark worked with a superintendent who understood his Artisan tendencies. The superintendent assumed the role of protector; he was the leader that Bennis and Biederman (1997) describe as keeping the wolves at bay so that another leader (Mark) can get the job done. The superintendent's role was to explain Mark's impatience to Guardian staff members and to soothe teachers and parents whose Guardian sensitivities had been violated.

Prior to unleashing Mark on a change process, the superintendent prepared school board members for the approaching storm. He described who might be upset and what they might be upset about, and outlined the probable step-by-step path of the approaching resistance, down to who the resistors might be and what they might be resisting. Then, as the change process unfolded, board members were comforted to know that the superintendent had a handle on the situation. Because the superintendent had somewhat removed himself from the fray, he was also able to act as a mediator for Mark when the staff or community needed a break from the tensions of the change process.

Unfortunately, when Mark became a superintendent himself, he no longer had a protector. Once again, people greeted Mark with enthusiasm. They loved his sense of humor, his Southern charm, and his firm grasp of learning and teaching. As the school board gave Mark his orders for change, its members assured him that they would stand behind his decisions. Key staff members also pledged their support. They told him they knew that the changes would be difficult but that the vast majority of parents and staff would support the changes once they understood them. But without a second leader to protect him from the wolves, Mark was fired before the end of his first year on the job.

Explain, Model, Practice, and Protect

All leaders need to understand people's expectations, but they also need a road map to keep focused during difficult and emotional periods of change. As a school superintendent, Mark had responded effectively to his school board's expectations. His board, like many others across the United States, was simply not willing to take the heat.

There are, however, exceptions to this rule. As Negroni (2000), a Massachusetts superintendent, suggests, when school leaders see the school board as individuals rather than as "the board," they can build a common purpose with seven other people who have similar goals. Goals become more important than positions. Greely (2000), a California school board member, says, "When I took office on the school board, I assumed I would have a lot to learn about education. But I soon discovered I had a lot to learn about how organizations work, how schools are governed, and why the barriers to change exist."

Greely addresses the impact of state funding, testing, political agendas, and open meeting laws on a school board's ability to be a learning team. She suggests the following six steps to help school board members move beyond these constraints. Following each step, I have added a reference to concepts mentioned earlier in this book.

- *Create a public record of your private conversations.* This is similar to the weekly memo from the superintendent to the school board. This way, everyone receives the same information.
- *Resist the temptation to invoke business examples.* As with the critical questions mentioned earlier, this puts the focus on learning rather than telling.
- *Keep returning to the observable data.* Be data-driven. Instead of citing "numerous" concerns, say how many people actually raised the issue.
- *Set up alternative meeting formats.* These are similar to the community dialogues mentioned earlier.

- *Practice talking about values.* Remind yourself of the purpose (in terms of student achievement and well-being) behind the practice.
- *Have your behavior as a board model the behavior you want from the schools.* All learners learn from daily models.

Districtwide protocols help stakeholders understand and implement change in a focused and consistent manner across groups and communities. They provide concrete mechanisms for stakeholders to understand the Four *P*s and lead to an expectation that everyone is responsible for success.

Distinguishing Between Personal Comfort and Organizational Purpose

Expecting everyone to be responsible for the Four *P*s is a matter of integrity, but integrity is not always synonymous with comfort. Again, Bennis (1989) describes trust as "walking your talk," whereas integrity is "talking your walk." Effective leaders need to communicate what they are really doing rather than trying to follow idealistic but unachievable principles. Let's consider what integrity looks like in a school environment.

One of the most common criticisms of public schools is the lack of accountability. Two examples often cited are tenure and a pay system based on years of service rather than merit. New school board members often push a superintendent to "fix" this problem through negotiations. School administrators spend hours discussing weak attempts at reform. State legislators expend a great deal of political capital trying to legislate changes at the state level. But these efforts have done little to change evaluations and pay schedules, and they have diverted a considerable amount of energy from the real task at hand—improving student achievement and well-being.

In a Guardian environment, change sometimes comes more easily when it happens to someone else. As the Four *P*s emerged in Thompson School District, it became obvious that the procedures for staff evaluations tied to salary were inconsistent with district expectations. Several board members and district administrators wanted to approach the teachers' association president about changing the evaluation process. They were finally convinced that the best way to encourage such change was to model it. With the help of the Colorado Association of School Boards, the board worked for almost 18 months to revise the superintendent's evaluation process.

Money is not always a school leader's primary motivator. Consequently, a point system based on merit can be more than ineffective; it can be counterproductive. To determine the important evaluation factors for motivating your leaders, you might want to ask the following critical questions:

- How does the evaluation align with the district's strategic goals?
- How could we use the evaluation process to monitor the change process on a year-to-year basis?
- What kinds of feedback would be most beneficial in keeping the board informed and involved and in keeping leaders motivated and effective?

Creating pathways for people to become intimately involved with your schools is merely the first step to renewal. The next question is "How do you deal with the natural tendency to form a new 'good old boys' network?" Omotani (2000), an Iowa school superintendent, invites the community into the process by creating larger teams that include parents and business leaders. He guides their participation by encouraging each school site to create its own set of goals consistent with district goals and insisting that they revisit guiding principles that underlie these goals on a regular basis. He understands that communities have changed. Parents have more choices today, and with expanding technologies, their decisions can have a significant impact on their children's progress in school.

Molly, the parent of a 5-year-old, met with her school superintendent to inquire about his vision for the school district. Following their conversation, the superintendent asked Molly why she had come to him rather than the teacher or the principal at the school. Molly's response was, "Oh, I've toured the school with the principal and visited several kindergarten classrooms, but

I want to know what my daughter's education will look like over the next 13 years, not just in kindergarten."

Varying Organizational Activities and Assigning Tasks to Suit People's Talents

Earlier we indicated that a liability is little more than a strength that is carried too far. Guardians dominate the school culture, and with this domination come both strengths and liabilities. Guardian strengths include teamwork, stability, and consistency. Carried too far, these strengths can turn into liabilities: groupthink, monotony, and boredom. Sherry, a school district communications official, put it best: "I'd like to take more risks in my life, if I could only be certain they'd work out."

When a school district fully implements the Four *P*s, it can explore possibilities without putting children at risk. The Four *P*s begin with a clear understanding of purpose and parameters (strategic goals and decision-making procedures). However, these first two *P*s are dynamic. The district's strategic goals remain constant over the long term, but the tasks necessary to accomplish them vary from year to year. Leaders ask, "Can you describe what that goal looks like today in this setting? Given how far we have come and what we know about our students, where do we go from here?"

Effective leaders encourage parents and staff to discuss these questions together. Because they have a clear understanding of who makes what decisions, they can focus on students' needs rather than on power politics. They can establish future directions together and use the remaining *P*s (principles and priorities) to pilot adjustments in programs and services before committing long-term resources. Figure 6.4 lists several keys to leading within the Four *P*s.

The key to leadership within the Four *P*s is to refrain from substituting Rational analysis and Artisan action for Guardian stability and Idealist human relationships. It is necessary to balance these four personality characteristics. Cultures exist to meet human needs and expectations. They flourish when they remain open to new ideas without losing sight of their original purpose. It is not easy to manage Rationals and Artisans. Rationals ask questions that

FIGURE 6.4
Keys to Leading with the Four *P*s

- Be certain that questions regarding why a program or service is important can be answered in terms of what students need to know and be able to do.
- Listen to everyone, but listen more to those who have expertise or accountability in a particular area.
- Think of principles as purpose-in-action. Honor people's right to be wrong.
- Assign resources to programs and services that work, not those that people think should work.

people sometimes don't want to consider. They question the logic of programs and services and point out inconsistencies between what people espouse and what they practice. Artisans crave uniqueness. They test limits and need frequent recognition of their accomplishments. Guardians, however, often lament what should have been instead of responding to what *is*. Idealists try so hard to make personal connections that they can lose sight of expectations.

The assumption underlying shared decision making is that having more people involved increases the likelihood of making better decisions. But more opinions do not necessarily equate to more diverse opinions. People of like temperaments can give the impression of diversity based solely on the number of opinions involved. Guardians have different needs and fears depending on their experience and expertise. But their solutions have strikingly similar characteristics. They will be focused, rule driven, and designed to create a specific outcome or array of outcomes. Bob's efforts to hire a new middle school math teacher provide a good example of this.

Bob wanted to hire a teacher who was child centered and competent in math. But he also recognized that a successful teacher would need to work effectively with colleagues and get along with parents. In preparing for his search, Bob began by sitting with his math teachers to determine the kinds of skills they needed to complement their department. Next, he met with the 7th grade teachers with whom the new math teacher would team. Bob even asked members of the student government to help him identify teacher characteristics that students valued. Finally, he brought together an interview team consisting of one math teacher, two 7th grade teachers, a counselor, and two parents. After sharing the list of desirable characteristics he had compiled, Bob helped the team develop a set of interview questions and a rubric for evaluating candidates.

Bob and several math teachers conducted a paper screening of applicants. Then the committee interviewed five prospective math teachers. In the end, the committee screened the candidates down to two people: a veteran middle school teacher who was described as highly organized and effective, and a former accountant who had recently been certified to teach. Both seemed to be caring individuals, and both obviously knew their math.

During the debriefing with the committee, Bob received the following feedback:

Veteran teacher:

Strengths—is well organized, has good references, understands the middle school philosophy, stressed classroom management, spoke frequently about being a team player, has experience with technology

Weaknesses—has little experience with interdisciplinary teaming, did not have experience with portfolio assessment but expressed interest in learning

Former accountant:

Strengths—is creative and enthusiastic, spoke often of applying math to real life, has worked with accounting teams, stressed student interest and parent involvement, had designed accounting and communications software, was enthusiastic about what he had learned in his certification classes about child psychology

Weaknesses—has no real classroom experience, spoke too much about workplace skills, might be better suited for high school, has personal enthusiasm that might inhibit his ability to be a team player

In the end, the team, with the exception of Bob and one parent, agreed that the veteran teacher would be a safer bet. He was more of a known quantity. The former accountant had potential, but they all recalled an exuberant teacher they had hired a few years earlier who had turned out to be a bit of a rebel. He had motivated students, but his methods were unorthodox. He had opposed ability grouping of any kind, and he had been more concerned with pleasing parents than with supporting school rules.

If you look at these strengths and liabilities closely, the Guardian nature emerges clearly. Guardians go with the predictable over the unpredictable, the known average over the unknown possibilities. Guardian committee members want a teacher who will fit in, support school procedures, and be a team player. Differences engender doubts and pose potential challenges to "the way we do things around here."

One of the mistakes that many school leaders make today is to assume that including people from different departments and different stakeholder groups ensures different perspectives. Committees are neither good nor bad. Their success depends on their makeup, their purpose, their training, and their leadership. At the risk of seeming undemocratic and top-down, leaders must consider other means of engaging people in various problem-solving situations. Let's think about how Bob might have handled his hiring task differently.

Guardians want to be right. They ask their questions in terms of yes and no, right and wrong, and how many answers they got right. They seldom ask questions unless they know the answers. And they tend to look at questions from supervisors, especially open-ended questions, as threatening or challenging.

Bob was right to gather input from various stakeholder groups. His math teachers offered the expertise Bob needed to determine the candidates' content knowledge of mathematics. Teachers on the 7th grade team provided input on the types of team skills they needed to complement their own skills and interests. Students and parents provided insights into the characteristics that would address their own styles and interests. But in the end, Bob was the only person trained in interviewing techniques. He was the person who would have to supervise and evaluate the new math teacher. And Bob had the added advantage of being the only person with responsibilities to all of the other stakeholder groups. Bob was ultimately the person accountable for the new math teacher's success or failure.

Bob might have gathered all the same information from the same groups but kept the interviewing responsibilities for himself. Because Bob had not taught mathematics, he might have included a math teacher in the interviews to assess answers to content knowledge questions. He might have trained a standing hiring committee with a member from each grade level and each department. Of equal importance, Bob might have interviewed students and parents from various subgroups—high-achieving, low-achieving, minorities, disadvantaged/at-risk, and so on—to determine the things that teachers did to help various students experience success.

Committees often serve more of a verification than a problem-solving function. Organizations can spend inordinate amounts of time arguing about committee size, composition, and authority; committees are often politically inspired and politically motivated. They can degenerate into a microcosm of the political differences within the greater organization. Leaders can use the guidelines listed in Figure 6.5 to improve the formation and effectiveness of committees.

Committees take time to form and time to work together before they can achieve any level of effectiveness or efficiency. They are more effective as tools for investigation and input than as decision-making bodies. Committees should not become substitutes for defining a clear line of accountability and communication. Leaders need to develop trust through the results of their actions over time. Committees and task forces involve people, but your stakeholders do not have to be directly involved in every aspect of every task. That degree of involvement can become inefficient, exhausting, and frustrating to everyone.

Finding a Dynamic Balance

It is neither necessary nor desirable to change the personality of a school district through hiring practices. Nor is it possible to guarantee the personality

FIGURE 6.5
To Committee or Not to Committee

To determine whether or not to form a committee, leaders should

- Determine the specific perspectives that can enhance problem solving in this area;
- Determine which stakeholder groups are involved and to what extent they have a direct customer- or accountability-related perspective;
- Determine how much time is available for selecting, training, and supporting a committee compared to the magnitude of the problem at hand and the outcome likely to result from the committee's work;
- Determine what other methods of data gathering might be used along with the practical and political impact of each; and
- Make certain that, if a committee is to be formed, stakeholders have a clear outline of their task and authority.

balance of every school team, department, or committee. It is possible, however, to build balance into the organizational culture. By following the Four *P*s, leaders can nurture balanced leadership throughout a school district.

Power exists in all parts of a school community, but authority rests primarily with the school board and the administration. They must initiate and model the Four *P*s in order to create an expectation for their use across organizational structures. They need to make frequent references to the strategic plan in meeting agendas and informal conversations, and to demonstrate shared decision making through their own community dialogues and meeting procedures. They need to ask administrators to restate the purpose of various committees and task forces in their own words, explaining who is involved and how they are involved. They need to ask how programs and services will be evaluated, what success looks like, and how resources may be reallocated to replicate successful practices.

Wayne holds three monthly meetings with his school board. One meeting, called a "study session," focuses on in-depth discussions of one or two topics. Study session topics typically include tasks from the yearly responsibility matrix, such as minority achievement, summaries of action plans by level, updates on the technology plan, midyear progress reports, and budget. No action takes place at these study sessions. They provide opportunities for the school board to gain new information, ask questions, and provide direction to the superintendent and his staff. The other two monthly board meetings are each divided into two parts: action and discussion. Items discussed at one meeting typically appear on the next meeting's agenda for action.

Wayne's executive team meets twice a month to reflect on long-term strategic issues and once a month to discuss the nuts-and-bolts tasks necessary to achieve those strategic purposes. Principals and other middle managers meet once each month as a whole group to receive updates of school board actions and to participate in professional development activities. They meet by level or division twice a month to discuss common issues and to ensure program articulation by level. Then once each month, principals and district office staff participate as an ongoing learning community in researching and honing skills that they have identified for growth and development. Professional development topics have included developing a balanced mathematics program, effective meeting/discussion protocols to improve participation, developing a special education support and intervention team, and creating a discipline grid to ensure due process in student discipline.

There is nothing magical or especially unique about school board and executive meetings of this nature. Their significance lies in their intent: to model balanced leadership based on the Four *P*s. Some people are extremely skilled at making connections with others but lack the focus they need to act effectively and bring closure to a meeting or project; others can bring tremendous focus to a topic, but fail to see its connection to another topic or process. Some people are great systems analysts, but find it difficult to make decisions without gathering more information.

It takes many people to make a school district successful. Those people need to have a common purpose, an agreed-upon set of decision-making parameters, a process for monitoring their progress, and a plan for effectively allocating their resources.

Dealing with the Pains of Leadership

Effective leaders are often lonely people. It is far easier to win friends and admirers by focusing on the needs of a few influential stakeholder groups than by grappling with complex problems that some people don't even know they have and many don't want to admit. It is far easier to become a hero by focusing on the needs of the oppressed than by grappling with the seemingly mundane problems of the masses. To not only survive but thrive amid the perils of leadership, you need to have practical tools for steering a balanced course—a course that is both stable and flexible, both sensible and systematic. Figure 6.6 provides guidelines for developing and nurturing leadership in your school district.

Make certain that your leaders appreciate and openly honor past achievements within their school or department. It is far easier to get people to think about where they will go next (to reframe their target) than to convince them that they have totally missed the mark in the past and need to

	FIGURE 6.6 How to Develop and Nurture Leadership

Help stakeholders learn to

Reframe the organizational *purpose* through various tasks and across organizational structures.

Evaluate decision-making *parameters* according to their fit with the organizational purpose across committees and task forces.

Analyze student achievement data in terms of established *principles* that define success for all student groups within and across organizational structures.

Leverage resources toward *priorities* based on programs and services that work over time and across groups and communities.

create a totally new direction. Make certain that your leaders know how to evaluate programs and services in terms of organizational purpose rather than in terms of philosophical or political agendas, and that your leaders have a deep commitment and an abiding focus on the guiding principle of education in a democracy—educating all students to their fullest potential. Make sure that your leaders appreciate the need for flexibility in leveraging resources toward effective programs and services rather than perpetuating the status quo.

If you are an Idealist, it is not easy to make decisions that strain relationships and test people's comfort levels. If you are a Rational, it is not easy to accept political expediency that falls short of logical consistencies. If you are an Artisan, it is not easy to deal with the slow pace of consensus building necessary to move an entire school district. If you are a Guardian, it is not easy to accept solutions, no matter how good they may be, if they do not emerge through established guidelines and procedures. But as stakeholders make the Four Ps a habit, they will begin to see that reasonable flexibility can occur within a stable environment and that they can make data-driven decisions without losing sight of the relationships that make them a community.

A learning community is an ever-changing body. Wheatley (1992) suggests that communities break down parameters from time to time only to rebuild them on a higher level. The Four Ps allow leaders to make this happen with a bit less chaos. Even balanced leaders cannot anticipate all the possible risks and twists and turns that await in a change process. However, when people use the Four Ps to plan for, implement, and adjust such a process, their chances of success multiply at least fourfold. You and your stakeholders cannot control change, but you can engage in it together.

Take a moment to answer the following questions to assess your Four P inventory:

1. What is your vision of a quality school experience?
   a. What are students doing and saying that demonstrates an enthusiasm for learning?

b. How are parents and community members participating in your school(s), and what are they saying about the quality of the school(s)?

c. How are teachers talking about and planning for learning? Are they excited and enthusiastic or feeling overburdened?

d. How are administrators encouraging inquiry and reflection through staff and community dialogues?

2. How have you used your vision of quality as a catalyst to encourage spirited discussions about the purpose of schooling?

3. How do various stakeholders within your school community describe the atmosphere for change? Is it happening to them or with them?

4. To what extent have you achieved the Four *P* balance in the following realms?

a. Answering questions regarding programs and services in terms of what students need to know and be able to do.

b. Listening to everyone, but listening more to those who have expertise or accountability in a particular area.

c. Thinking of principles as purpose-in-action and honoring people's right to be wrong.

d. Assigning resources to programs and services that work, not those that people think should work.

Conclusion

Stacey is 27 years old and about to enter a 30-day drug and alcohol rehabilitation program. Though his problems started in middle school, he is one of the lucky ones. Unlike the families of many students who do not find success in school, Stacey's family stuck with him, waiting for him to find a reason to believe in himself. But what happens to the Staceys whose families believe that their responsibilities end at adolescence—or earlier?

A great deal of what we believe about learning and about ourselves as learners is derived from our school experiences. This is not to say that Stacey's problems are someone else's fault; he had caring teachers and parents. But most public schools expect students to fit in, to learn the way teachers teach. That is not our stated purpose, but far too often it describes the day-to-day reality within the school walls.

Tomorrow's democracy will be as strong as today's public schools. If we continue providing the same input, we will continue to get the same results. We will not close the various achievement gaps that exist, and we will become a society of haves and have-nots.

Public schools are a life-shaping experience. They have a tremendous effect on an individual's self-image. Making every student a successful learner is therefore not just a desirable goal, but a moral obligation. It is an absolute necessity for maintaining our democracy.

Students learn more from what we as adults do—what we model—than from what we say. As educators, we must practice our mission on a daily basis, make information available to every stakeholder, and create schools where adults honor differences, from the classroom to the boardroom. The measure of a good decision is the extent to which it makes programs and services accessible to all students.

As a school leader you can use the following steps to build and sustain such schools:

- Understand the quality profile so that the personality of your school district honors and responds to the personality of your community as a whole.
- Ask quality questions that promote understanding and individual growth rather than define success as a process of following the rules.
- Make quality a habit by creating organizational structures that address the Four *P*s—purpose, parameters, principles, and priorities— on an ongoing basis.
- Focus on success as a means of renewing schools from within rather than imposing solutions that cannot be sustained over time and across groups and communities.
- Manage tasks so that people learn to solve problems together and, in the process, learn to appreciate different personalities as a valuable part of problem solving.

You can build a balanced organizational structure within your school community. You can help students and parents become valued participants within that structure. You can close the gap between your school district's stated purpose and its day-to-day actions by nurturing leaders who ask the Four *P* questions:

- *Purpose:* Why is this program or service important for student achievement and well-being?
- *Parameters:* How will we make day-to-day decisions that create quality schools and ensure success for *all* students?
- *Principles:* Do we hold ourselves accountable for ensuring that our programs and services actually achieve our stated purpose?
- *Priorities:* Do we identify funding priorities in terms of programs and services that work (success for whom, under what circumstances, given what evidence)?

Knowledge and skills are important. But students must have a reasonable expectation of success in order to enjoy learning and to believe in their ability to learn. Students learn those expectations from their adult role models. The Four *P*s alone will not make every student successful. They can, however, help parents and educators build connections with one another and with their children. You may be surprised at how many successful programs and services already exist in your school district when you begin to look for them. Remember, quality is a shifting target. You and your stakeholders should decide when to move that target rather than wait for others to move it for you.

References

Bennis, W. (1989). *On becoming a leader*. Reading, MA: Addison-Wesley.

Bennis, W., & Biederman, P. (1997). *Organizing genius: The secrets of creative collaboration*. Reading, MA: Addison-Wesley.

Bolman, L., & Deal, T. (1984). *Modern approaches to understanding and managing organizations*. San Francisco: Jossey-Bass.

Bolman, L., & Deal, T. (1997). *Reframing organizations: Artistry, choice, and leadership*. San Francisco: Jossey-Bass.

Bridges, W. (1991). *Managing transitions: Making the most of change*. Reading, MA: Addison-Wesley.

Bruner, J., & Bornstein, M. (1989). On interaction. In M. Bornstein & J. Bruner (Eds.), *Interaction in human development*. Hillsdale, NJ: L. Erlbaum Associates.

Caine, R. N., & Caine, G. (1991). *Making connections: Teaching and the human brain*. Alexandria, VA: Association for Supervision and Curriculum Development.

Chrislip, D. (2002). *The collaborative leadership fieldbook: A guide for citizens and civic leaders*. San Francisco: Jossey-Bass.

Clark, R., & Hughes, D. (1995). *Partner schools: Definitions and expectations* (rev. ed.). Seattle: Center for Educational Renewal, University of Washington.

Costa, A. (Ed.). (2001). *Developing minds: A resource book for teaching thinking*. Alexandria, VA: Association for Supervision and Curriculum Development.

Csikszentmihalyi, M. (1990). *Flow: The psychology of optimal experience*. New York: Harper & Row.

Danielson, C. (2002). *Enhancing student achievement: A framework for school improvement*. Alexandria, VA: Association for Supervision and Curriculum Development.

Dolan, P. (1994). *Restructuring our schools: A primer on systemic change*. Kansas City, MO: Systems & Organization.

Frankl, V. (1959). *Man's search for meaning: An introduction to logotherapy.* New York: Simon and Schuster.

Galpin, T. (1996). *The human side of change: A practical guide to organization redesign.* San Francisco: Jossey-Bass.

Gardner, H. (1993). *Multiple intelligences: The theory in practice.* New York: Basic Books.

Goldberg, M., & Feldman, S. (2003). *Teachers with class: True stories of great teachers.* Kansas City, MO: Andrews McMeel Publishing.

Goodlad, J. (2004). *Romances with schools: A life of education.* New York: McGraw-Hill.

Goodlad, J., Mantle-Bromley, C., & Goodlad, S. (2004). *Education for everyone: Agenda for education in a democracy.* San Francisco: Jossey-Bass.

Greely, G. (2000). A school board that learns. In P. Senge, et al., *Schools that learn: A fifth discipline fieldbook for educators, parents, and everyone who cares about education.* New York: Doubleday.

Hart, L. (1983). *Human brain, human learning.* New York: Longman.

Hartzler, M., & Henry, J. (1994). *Team fitness: A how-to manual for building a winning work team.* Milwaukee, WI: ASQC Quality Press.

Heifetz, R. (1994). *Leadership without easy answers.* Cambridge, MA: Harvard University Press.

Hiebert, J., Carpenter, T., Fennema, E., Fuson, K., Wearne, D., Murray, H., Oliver, A., & Human, P. (1997). *Making sense: Teaching and learning mathematics with understanding.* Portsmouth, NH: Heinemann.

Hodgkinson, H. (2003). *Leaving too many children behind: A demographer's view on the neglect of America's youngest children.* Washington, DC: The Institute for Educational Leadership.

Holcomb, E. (1999). *Getting excited about data: How to combine people, passion, and proof.* Thousand Oaks, CA: Corwin Press.

Holcomb, E. (2001). *Asking the right questions: Techniques for collaboration and school change.* Thousand Oaks, CA: Corwin Press.

Hunter, M. (1969). *Improved instruction.* Thousand Oaks, CA: Corwin Press.

Johnson, D. (1980). *A comprehensive study of a systematic needs assessment in a small rural middle school.* Unpublished doctoral dissertation. University of Pittsburgh, Pittsburgh.

Johnson, D. (1999). *Engaging with change: The need for compassion in school reform.* Plymouth, VT: Five Corners Publications.

Johnson. D. (2004). *The real colors homeowner's guide.* Phoenix, AZ: National Curriculum and Training Institute.

Keirsey, D., & Bates, M. (1978). *Please understand me: Character and temperament types.* Del Mar, CA: Prometheus Nemesis Books.

Keirsey, D., & Bates, M. (1998). *Please understand me II: Temperament, character, intelligence.* Del Mar, CA: Prometheus Nemesis Books.

Kroeze, D., & Johnson, D. (1997). *Achieving excellence: A report of initial findings from the Third International Mathematics and Science Study.* Northbrook, IL: First in the World Consortium.

Levine, M. (2002). *A mind at a time.* New York: Simon & Schuster.

Lieberman, A., & Grolnick, M. (1997). Networks, reform, and the professional development of teachers. In A. Hargreaves (Ed.), *Rethinking educational change with heart and mind.* Alexandria, VA: Association for Supervision and Curriculum Development.

Marzano, R. (1988). *Dimensions of thinking: A framework for curriculum and instruction.* Alexandria, VA: Association for Supervision and Curriculum Development.

Marzano, R. (2003). *What works in schools: Translating research into action.* Alexandria, VA: Association for Supervision and Curriculum Development.

Marzano, R., Pickering, D. J., & Pollock, J. E. (2001). *Classroom instruction that works: Research-based strategies for increasing student achievement.* Alexandria, VA: Association for Supervision and Curriculum Development.

Merriam-Webster's ninth new collegiate dictionary. (1991). Springfield, MA: Merriam-Webster.

Myers, I. (1962). *Manual: The Myers-Briggs type indicator.* Palo Alto, CA: Consulting Psychologists Press.

Myers, I., & McCaulley, M. (1985). *Manual: A guide to the development and use of the Myers-Briggs type indicator.* Palo Alto, CA: Consulting Psychologists Press.

National Curriculum and Training Institute. (1995). *Real colors.* Phoenix, AZ: National Curriculum and Training Institute.

Negroni, P. (2000). The superintendent's progress. In P. Senge et al., *Schools that learn: A fifth discipline fieldbook for educators, parents, and everyone who cares about education.* New York: Doubleday.

Omotani, L. (2000). As the community goes, so goes the school. In P. Senge et al., *Schools that learn: A fifth discipline fieldbook for educators, parents, and everyone who cares about education.* New York: Doubleday.

Paul, R., & Elder, L. (2002). *Critical thinking: Tools for taking charge of your professional and personal life.* Upper Saddle River, NJ: Prentice-Hall.

Peale, N. (1974). *You can if you think you can.* Englewood Cliffs, NJ: Prentice-Hall.

Phye, G. (1997). Classroom assessment: A multidimensional perspective. In G. Phye (Ed.), *Handbook of classroom assessment: Learning, achievement, and adjustment.* San Diego: Academic Press.

Piaget, J. (1952). *The origins of intelligence in children* (M. Cook, Trans.). New York: International Universities Press.

Piaget, J. (1977). *The development of thought: Equilibration of cognitive structures* (A. Rosin, Trans.). New York: Viking Press.

Quinn, R. (1996). *Deep change: Discovering the leader within.* San Francisco: Jossey-Bass.

Roberts, C. (2000). Leading without control. In P. Senge et al., *Schools that learn: A fifth discipline fieldbook for educators, parents, and everyone who cares about education.* New York: Doubleday.

Saban. J., Killion, J., & Green, C. (1994). The centric reflection model: A kaleidoscope for staff developers. *Journal of Staff Development, 15*(3), 16–20.

Schön, D. (1983). *The reflective practitioner: How professionals think in action.* New York: Basic Books.

Senge, P. (1990). *The fifth discipline: The art and practice of the learning organization.* New York: Doubleday/Currency.

Senge, P., Cambron-McCabe, N., Lucas, T., Smith, B., Dutton, J., & Kleiner, A. (2000). *Schools that learn: A fifth discipline fieldbook for educators, parents, and everyone who cares about education.* New York: Doubleday.

Skinner, B. F. (1948). *Walden two.* New York: Macmillan.

Skinner, B. F. (1968). *The technology of teaching.* New York: Appleton-Century Crofts.

Toffler, A. (1970). *Future shock.* New York: Random House.

Tyack, D., & Cuban, L. (1995). *Tinkering toward utopia: A century of public school reform.* Cambridge, MA: Harvard University Press.

Wheatley, M. (1992). *Leadership and the new science: Learning about organization from an orderly universe.* San Francisco: Berrett-Koehler Publishers.

Index

Note: Page numbers followed by *f* refer to figures.

About the Author

Daniel P. Johnson is Superintendent of the Thompson School District in Loveland, Colorado. A 35-year veteran of education, he has written and conducted numerous workshops about the use of temperament as a leadership tool in large organizations.

In the mid-1990s, Johnson worked extensively with a group of suburban school districts that participated in the Third International Mathematics and Science Study (TIMSS). In this book, he combines his TIMSS research with his knowledge of temperament to suggest five practical steps that school leaders can use to create and sustain quality public schools. Johnson can be contacted by telephone at 970-622-9531 or by e-mail at johnsonda@thompson.k12.co.us.

Related ASCD Resources

Sustaining Change in Schools: How to Overcome Differences and Focus on Quality

At the time of publication, the following ASCD resources were available; for the most up-to-date information about ASCD resources, go to www.ascd.org. ASCD stock numbers are noted in parentheses.

Audio

Bringing Everybody on Board: Seven Keys to Unlocking Change by Todd Whitaker (Audiotape #504338)

Changing Schools Through Changing Leadership by Kathy O'Neill (Audiotape #204253)

Mars and Venus in the Board Room: Principles of Leadership from Male and Female Perspectives by Lydia Begley and Carl Bonuso (Audiotape #203134)

Shared Governance, Collaboration, and Student Achievement: What is the Connection? by Bob Ewy (Audiotape #204089)

Books

Analytic Processes for School Leaders by Cynthia T. Richetti and Benjamin B. Tregoe (#101017)

Leadership Capacity for Lasting School Improvement by Linda Lambert (#102283)

Professional Learning Communities at Work: Best Practices for Enhancing Student Achievement by Richard Dufour and Robert Eaker (#198188)

Transforming Schools: Creating a Culture of Continuous Improvement by Allison Zmuda, Robert Kuklis, and Everett Kline (#103112)

Multimedia

Creating the Capacity for Change by Jody Mason Westbrook and Valarie Spiser-Albert (ASCD Action Tool #702118)

Guide for Instructional Leaders by Roland Barth, Bobb Darnell, Laura Lipton, and Bruce Wellman (ASCD Action Tool #702110)

For more information, visit us on the World Wide Web (http://www.ascd.org), send an e-mail message to member@ascd.org, call the ASCD Service Center (1-800-933-ASCD or 703-578-9600, then press 2), send a fax to 703-575-5400, or write to Information Services, ASCD, 1703 N. Beauregard St., Alexandria, VA 22311-1714 USA.